Collins

Key Stage 3
Medieval
British and World History
410–1509
2nd edition
Laura Aitken-Burt, Robert Peal and Robert Selth

T0340466

William Collins' dream of knowledge for all began with the publication of his first book in 1819. A self-educated mill worker, he not only enriched millions of lives, but also founded a flourishing publishing house. Today, staying true to this spirit, Collins books are packed with inspiration, innovation and practical expertise. They place you at the centre of a world of possibility and give you exactly what you need to explore it.

Collins. Freedom to teach

Published by Collins
An imprint of HarperCollins*Publishers*
The News Building, 1 London Bridge Street, London, SE1 9GF, UK

HarperCollins*Publishers* Macken House,
39/40 Mayor Street Upper, Dublin 1, D01 C9W8, Ireland

Browse the complete Collins catalogue at
collins.co.uk

ISBN 978-0-00-849204-5

British Library Cataloguing-in-Publication Data
A catalogue record for this publication is available from the British Library.

Authors: Laura Aitken-Burt, Robert Peal and Robert Selth
Series editor: Robert Peal
Publisher: Katie Sergeant
Product manager: Joanna Ramsay
Editors: Caroline Low and Dawn Booth
Fact-checker: Barbara Hibbert
Proof-reader: David Hemsley
Cover designer: Gordon MacGilp
Cover image: Heritage Image Partnership Ltd / Alamy
Typesetter: QBS
Production controller: Alhady Ali
Printed and bound by
Ashford Colour Press Ltd

This book is produced from independently certified FSC™ paper to ensure responsible forest management.

For more information visit:
www.harpercollins.co.uk/green

Acknowledgements
The publishers gratefully acknowledge the permission granted to reproduce the copyright material in this book. Every effort has been made to trace copyright holders and to obtain their permission for the use of copyright material. The publishers will gladly receive any information enabling them to rectify any error or omission at the first opportunity.

Contents

Unit 7: The Crusades

Enquiry Question: *What motivated European knights to go on Crusade: God, greed or glory?*

Unit 8: Medieval African kingdoms

Enquiry question: *How did medieval African kingdoms wield their power?*

Unit 9: Imperial China

Enquiry Question: *Was Imperial China a place where nothing ever really changed, or a place of new beginnings?*

Unit 10: The Mongols

Enquiry Question: *How successful were the Mongols as conquerors and rulers?*

Introduction

'What I have always loved best about the history of the world is that it is true. That all the extraordinary things we read were no less real than you and I are today. What is more, what did happen is often far more exciting and amazing than anything we could invent.'

Ernst Gombrich, *A Little History of the World*

Book 1 of *Knowing History* begins with the departure of the Roman army from Britain in 410 AD, and ends around 1500. This is often known as the medieval period, meaning 'middle ages', because on a timeline it comes between Classical Rome and Greece, and the birth of the modern world. On this 1000-year journey, you will be transported to periods in the past that are both frightening and fascinating: from Viking invasions to medieval castles, from African Kingdoms to Mongol hordes.

The book is split evenly between British and World History, as both will help you to understand how the community in which you live today was formed. Within the British History units, you will learn how England first came to exist as a country, only to be conquered and ruled by a class of French knights. You will learn how medieval society developed and then was transformed by the Black Death. And you will learn how the people of medieval England believed with complete commitment in God, yet were capable of extraordinary cruelty – sometimes, even, in God's name.

The World History units span the Middle East, Africa and China. You will learn how Islam, now the second largest religion in the world, began in the Arabian town of Mecca around 610 CE. You will learn how the religions of Islam and Christianity clashed in their struggle for control of the Holy Land during the Crusades. You will travel to Africa, China and Central Asia to learn about medieval civilisations whose cultures and customs will seem both incredibly distant and strangely familiar.

You will visit the ruined castles and palaces, temples and cathedrals of the medieval period that still scatter the globe, and understand why they were built. The words that you hear around you fill with new meaning: pilgrims and peasants, monarchs and martyrs. And you will find inspiration in the lives lived by amazing individuals, such as Alfred the Great, Salah al-Din and Eleanor of Aquitaine.

The world today is as it is because of what has happened in the past. In studying history you may even start to see events in the present mirroring events in the past. As it is often said, history does not repeat itself, but it does sometimes rhyme.

Robert Peal, series editor and co-author of Knowing History

Concise **chapter introductions** set the scene for each topic.

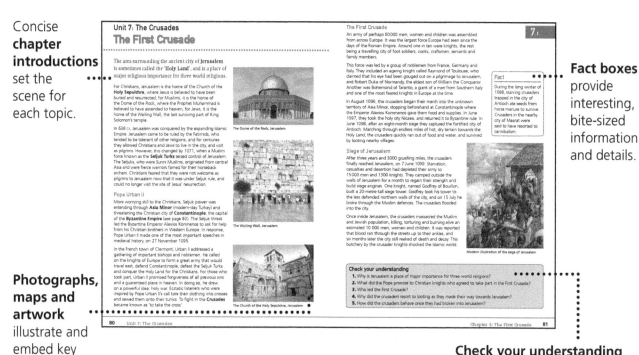

Fact boxes provide interesting, bite-sized information and details.

Photographs, maps and artwork illustrate and embed key concepts.

Check your understanding questions at the end of every chapter allow you to check and consolidate your learning.

Timelines map out the key dates from the unit, and help you understand the course of events. There is also a full timeline of events from across the units at the end of the book.

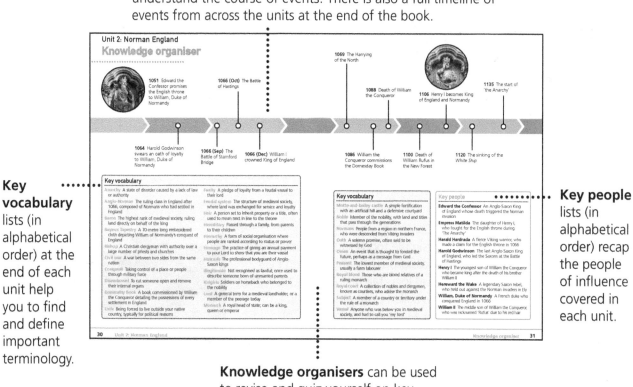

Key vocabulary lists (in alphabetical order) at the end of each unit help you to find and define important terminology.

Key people lists (in alphabetical order) recap the people of influence covered in each unit.

Knowledge organisers can be used to revise and quiz yourself on key dates, people and definitions.

Unit 1: Anglo-Saxon England

The Anglo-Saxons

The Romans ruled Britain for 400 years, until 410 AD, when the Roman army abandoned the country.

A population of remaining Roman civilians and **native** Britons – also known as '**Celts**' – were left to fend for themselves. Over the next two centuries, two tribes from northern Germany invaded Britain. Known as the **Anglo-Saxons**, they were fierce warriors who killed and enslaved the British population and remaining Romans.

The Anglo-Saxons took control of eastern and central England. Only Wales, Scotland and the West Country (Devon, Cornwall and Somerset) remained largely unaffected. Without the Roman army to defend against the Anglo-Saxon invaders, the culture and Christian religion of Roman society in Britain began to fade. Roman technologies such as glassmaking, road building and heated baths were lost.

Unlike the Romans, the early Anglo-Saxons could not read or write, and did not have the technology to build cities or roads. There are very few written records or buildings left from these early years of Anglo-Saxon rule for historians to study. For this reason, we know very little about what happened between the fifth and sixth centuries. This is one reason why some call this period the '**Dark Ages**'.

Britain was a very different place compared with today. There was a population of perhaps one million people living scattered across the countryside in villages and houses made of wood and straw. Most Anglo-Saxons lived in villages and small farming communities, and large parts of Roman towns such as Londinium (London) and Camulodunum (Colchester) were left to ruin.

Much of the countryside was covered in woodlands, where animals such as bears, wolves, wildcats and boar roamed. Other regions were covered in swamps and marshes. It was a mysterious land, where people told fantastic stories about dragons, wizards, monsters and giants.

Anglo-Saxon life

The Anglo-Saxon diet consisted of simple foods such as oats, beans and bread, and meat on special occasions. They also brewed beer from barley. Many Anglo-Saxons had long fair hair and the men grew beards. They made clothes out of woollen cloth and animal skin. They loved jewellery, and could make beautiful objects out of gold and gems. Both men and women fastened their clothing with gold brooches, which were a sign of power and wealth.

Most Anglo-Saxon men were farmers, but they were also warriors. In battle, they wore metal helmets, carried round wooden shields, and armed themselves with swords, throwing axes and

Recreation of an Anglo-Saxon village in West Stow, Suffolk, England

2-metre-long spears. An Anglo-Saxon man rarely went anywhere without being armed, as the need for protection was constant. Recently, chains and shackles from the Anglo-Saxon period have been found, telling us that the Anglo-Saxons enslaved people. These enslaved people might have been captured Celts, or criminals sentenced to slavery as punishment.

Anglo-Saxon treasure

As early Anglo-Saxons did not read or write, historians have very little evidence to learn more about the period. For this reason, the work of **archaeologists** is essential, and they have found some extraordinary Anglo-Saxon artefacts buried underground.

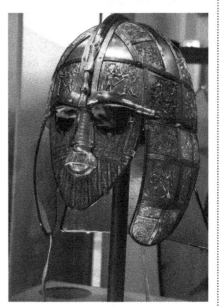

The most magnificent remains were found by the archaeologist Basil Brown in 1939 at a burial mound called **Sutton Hoo**. Here, he found the possessions of an Anglo-Saxon king, which had been buried in a ship so that he could take them to the afterlife. The king's possessions included:

- a golden purse lid decorated with wild animals and scenes such as wolves eating men

- two golden belt buckles (see top right)

- shoulder clasps for fastening clothing or armour decorated with wild boar

- weapons such as a shield, a sword and spear tips

- a small harp called a lyre

- silver plates and spoons that had been made in a far-off land called Byzantium (in modern-day Turkey)

- everyday objects, such as a feather cushion and combs made of antler horn.

Replica of the Sutton Hoo helmet made by the Royal Armories

The most famous find was a magnificent iron helmet with a patterned facemask. It was intricately decorated with scenes of war, such as a warrior on a horse trampling a fallen enemy. The treasures are thought to have belonged to Rædwald, the ruler of the Anglo-Saxon Kingdom of East Anglia who died in 624, but nobody knows for sure. Strangely, no body was ever found inside the burial mound.

The second greatest collection of Anglo-Saxon treasures was found in a Staffordshire field in 2009. Using his metal detector, a man named Terry Herbert uncovered 3500 gold and silver items, valued at over £3 million. You can be sure that more hoards of Anglo-Saxon treasure are still lying beneath the ground across England, waiting to be found.

Check your understanding

1. Who invaded Britain after the Roman army abandoned the country in 410 AD?
2. What sort of communities did Anglo-Saxons live in?
3. What sort of weapons did Anglo-Saxons use?
4. Why do historians know very little about life in early Anglo-Saxon Britain?
5. What was the most famous object found at Sutton Hoo?

Unit 1: Anglo-Saxon England
Anglo-Saxon rule

The Anglo-Saxon tribes who invaded Britain established a number of separate kingdoms across the country, each ruled by its own king.

By the end of the 7th **century** the three most powerful kingdoms were **Wessex**, **Mercia** and Northumbria, and rival kings often went to war against each other. Sometimes, one of the kings would become an 'overlord' with more power than all of the others.

The king lived in a Great Hall, built out of wood and straw, and showed his power by wearing a lot of gold jewellery. Life could be very violent, and Anglo-Saxons had to give their lives to defend their king. If they proved themselves to be loyal and brave in battle, they were rewarded with gold bracelets.

Anglo-Saxon place names

Many English place names come from old Anglo-Saxon words. For example, the word 'England' comes from '*Anglo*-land'. Today, the area where the Anglo-Saxons first settled in the east of England is called East Anglia, named after the Angles. Wessex, Essex and Sussex are named after the West, East and South Saxons. Also, Norfolk and Suffolk are named after the northern and southern people, or 'folk'.

The names for many English towns and cities still end in Anglo-Saxon words: 'don' means hill; 'ton' means house; 'ham' means village; 'wich' means farm; and 'ing' means people.

Anglo-Saxon religion

At first, the Anglo-Saxons were **pagans**, who believed in many different gods. Woden was the King of the Gods, but there was also Tiw the god of war, Freya the goddess of love and fertility, and Thor the god of thunder. The days of the week are still named after these gods today: Tiw became Tuesday, Woden became Wednesday, Thor became Thursday and Freya became Friday.

This pagan religion started to change when Pope Gregory in Rome sent a **monk** named Augustine to travel all the way to Britain, and convert the Anglo-Saxons to Christianity. Augustine landed on the south coast of England in 597 with a group of around 40 monks. Here, Augustine met Ethelbert, the King of Kent. Ethelbert's wife, a princess from France called Bertha, was already a Christian. Under Bertha and Augustine's influence, Ethelbert became the first Anglo-Saxon king to convert to Christianity.

Modern illustration of Saint Augustine meeting Ethelbert and Bertha

In 635, a monk called Aidan brought Christianity to Northumbria from Ireland. Aidan founded a **monastery** on a remote island called Lindisfarne, which became known as Holy Island. Kent and Northumbria became the centres of Christianity in England, from which this new religion eventually spread throughout the whole country. Today, we still have an **Archbishop of Canterbury** (in Kent) and an Archbishop of York (in what was Northumbria). Pope Gregory made Augustine the first Archbishop of Canterbury.

The written word

Christianity brought writing and study to England. Anglo-Saxon monks, who lived in monasteries built of stone, often dedicated their lives to study. They wrote magnificent manuscripts and Bibles by hand on **vellum** – a material made from the skin of calves. The most precious of these manuscripts were decorated with such bright colours that they were called '**illuminations**'. This is because they appeared to be lit up.

The most valuable historical source from this period was provided by a Northumbrian monk called Bede. When Bede was 7 years old, he was sent to be brought up in a monastery beside the River Tyne. Bede became a monk and decided to write down all of the stories about the Anglo-Saxon tribes and kings, which had been passed down through the generations in poem and song. In 731, Bede finished his great book, and called it *The Ecclesiastical History of the English People*. It was the first ever book of English history. Without it, we would know almost nothing about the early Anglo-Saxons. Bede's history was so well thought of that he became known as the 'Venerable' Bede, meaning respected.

Page from the Lindisfarne Gospels, an illuminated manuscript from the early 8th century

King Offa

One of the most famous Anglo-Saxon overlords was King Offa, who ruled Mercia between 757 and 796. Offa overpowered his rival kings, beheading those who rebelled against him.

To prevent the Welsh from invading his kingdom of Mercia, King Offa built a 149-mile-long earthwork between England and Wales, stretching from sea to sea. It was known as 'Offa's Dyke', and can still be seen running along the Welsh–English border today.

Fact

Pope Gregory advised Augustine to adapt Christianity to the Anglo-Saxons' pagan festivals. The term Easter comes from 'Eostre', the name of an Anglo-Saxon goddess of rebirth. Christmas is celebrated at around the time of the winter solstice, when the Anglo-Saxons celebrated their own festival called 'Yule'.

Check your understanding

1. How was England divided up during the early Anglo-Saxon period?
2. Which counties in England are named after the south, east and west Saxons?
3. How did four days of the week gain their names in the English language?
4. Why are Canterbury and York the two centres of English Christianity today?
5. Why is there more evidence about Anglo-Saxon life during the period after Christianity arrived?

Unit 1: Anglo-Saxon England
The Vikings

In January 793, a band of warriors attacked the Christian monastery on the Holy Island of Lindisfarne in Northumbria.

They arrived from the sea in ships with dragons' heads carved onto the bows, heavily armed with metal helmets, armour and two-handed axes. The warriors broke into the monastery, drowning the older monks in the sea and enslaving the younger monks. They then stole Lindisfarne's treasures, and sailed away.

For the next three centuries, Anglo-Saxon England was subject to repeated waves of attacks from these warriors. In particular, Christian monasteries, famous for their gold and precious treasures, were targeted. Who were these people? The Anglo-Saxons called them wolves of the sea, pagan people, Norsemen, Danes and stinging hornets. Today, they are better known as the **Vikings**.

Reconstruction of a Viking longboat

The Vikings

The Vikings came from the Scandinavian countries of Denmark, Norway and Sweden. They were skilled at building ships that used both oars and sails, and could therefore travel great distances by river and sea. Called **longboats**, these ships were a remarkable technology. They could hold up to 200 Viking warriors and sailed west as far as Canada, and east as far as Russia.

Some Vikings were traders, who brought spices, silks, wine and jewellery from distant lands. Others were raiders, who preferred killing and stealing to buying and selling. Viking warriors could be a terrifying sight: they wore animal skins, had tattoos, and some even filed their teeth to look more frightening in battle. Often, Anglo-Saxons would pay Viking invaders huge sums of money, known as the '**danegeld**', in return for the Vikings leaving them alone. However, once the danegeld had been paid the Vikings sometimes returned and attacked anyway.

There were few more terrifying sights for a coastal Anglo-Saxon town than the dragon head of a longboat looming into view. After the attack on Lindisfarne, a scholar named Alcuin of York wrote to the King of Northumbria: "Lo, it is nearly 350 years that we and our fathers have inhabited this most lovely land, and never before has such a terror appeared as we have now suffered from a pagan race. Behold the church of St Cuthbert spattered with the blood of the priests of God, despoiled of all its ornaments."

Viking settlement

At first, Vikings were content with hit-and-run raids on English coastal towns. However, in 865, the Vikings assembled a force to settle in England, known as the '**Great Heathen Army**'. It was led by the three sons of a Viking king named Ragnar Lodbrok. They were called Halfdan

Viking sword

Ragnarsson, Ivar the Boneless and Ubba. Nobody knows how large the army was, but estimates range from 1000 to 6000.

The three brothers captured the city of York in 867, and used it as a base to spread their power throughout northern England. Known as '**Jorvik**' to the Vikings, York became a thriving centre of overseas trade under Viking rule, and home to perhaps 15 000 people. Modern archaeological digs in York have found leather shoes, iron padlocks, coloured glass beads and ice skates made out of horse bone.

In 869, the Great Heathen Army advanced south, and attacked Edmund, the Anglo-Saxon King of East Anglia. He was captured by the Vikings, and refused to renounce his belief in Christianity. In return, a band of Vikings tied him to a tree and fired arrows at him until he, according to legend, "bristled with them like a hedgehog".

The Vikings' progress through Britain would have been violent, but they also assimilated and inter-married with the existing Anglo-Saxon population.

Valhalla

One reason why Vikings fought so fiercely was because of their belief that if they died in battle they would be taken to the glorious Viking heaven of **Valhalla**. This was a Great Hall ruled by Odin, the King of the Gods.

Vikings believed that Odin's female spirits, called Valkyries, carried warriors from the battlefield to Valhalla, where their wounds would be healed. In the evening, the warriors would feast on an enormous wild boar, which would be brought back to life each day. They would drink from a goat whose udders provided an unlimited supply of mead (beer). By day, the Viking would train to fight for Odin in a final battle of the gods, known as 'Ragnarok'.

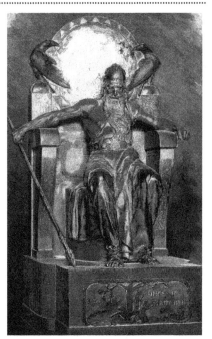

Modern illustration of Odin, King of the Gods

Fact

In one 11th-century Viking saga, a savage method for killing an Anglo-Saxon King of Northumbria was recorded. Known as the '**Blood Eagle**', it involved ripping the victim's lungs out of his body and draping them over his shoulders to resemble an eagle's folded wings.

Shield Maidens

Stories in Norse sagas tell of powerful 'shield maidens', such as Ragnar Lodbrok's wife Lagertha and Sigrid the Proud. Archaeological discoveries have recently shown women buried with weapons at Birka (Sweden) and in huge ships at Oseburg (Norway).

Check your understanding

1. Why did Viking raiders target Christian monasteries?
2. Why was the longboat so important to the Vikings?
3. How large was the Great Heathen Army thought to have been?
4. What did Vikings believe awaited them if they died in battle?
5. What city became the centre of Viking power in England?

Alfred the Great

Alfred was born the youngest of five sons to the King of Wessex. By the age of 23 his four brothers had all died, and in 871 Alfred became king.

King Alfred was immediately thrown into the long-running war between Wessex and the Viking Great Heathen Army, who had by now settled throughout much of England. During his first year as king, Alfred fought nine battles defending Wessex against the Vikings. He finally negotiated a truce: in return for a large danegeld payment, the Vikings agreed not to attack Wessex for 5 years.

However, a new Viking leader named King Guthrum wanted to take Wessex for himself. In 878, Guthrum's Viking army attacked King Alfred in Chippenham while he was celebrating Twelfth Night, the last day of Christmas.

Alfred and his men were caught by surprise. Many were slaughtered, but Alfred and a small band of men escaped and fled west towards the marshes of Somerset. Here they hid from Guthrum's army, and began to organise their counter-attack. Alfred knew the marshes well. He set up camp on Athelney, an island of high and dry land surrounded by swamp, from which he organised hit-and-run attacks on the Viking camps. He also began to raise a new army from the surrounding counties, which assembled at an ancient meeting point called Egbert's Stone in May 878. From there, they marched to meet Guthrum's Viking army at the Battle of Edington, where Alfred defeated the Vikings.

Guthrum was captured at Edington. However, instead of killing Guthrum, Alfred forced him to be baptised and convert to Christianity. Alfred even made himself Guthrum's godfather! Alfred and Guthrum agreed to divide England by a diagonal line from the mouth of the River Mersey in the north-west, to the mouth of the Thames in the south-east. The Vikings ruled land north of this line, and it was called the **Danelaw**.

Alfred as king

As a young boy, Alfred travelled to Rome with his father. Here he was inspired to be a great king, like a Roman Emperor. Having won his kingdom back from the Vikings, Alfred set about achieving this vision.

He built a series of around 30 fortress towns throughout Wessex known as **burhs** (or boroughs). In London, Alfred rebuilt the city walls that had fallen into ruin since the time of the Romans. Alfred also organised the **fyrd**: a part-time Anglo-Saxon army that could be called up to fight at times of war. Most importantly, he established a naval force, which sailed around the country protecting it from further attacks from Viking longships.

Statue of King Alfred built in the old Wessex capital of Winchester to celebrate the 1000-year anniversary of his death

This gold and enamel jewel was found in 1693 near Athelney. Around the edge of the gold frame is written in Old English, 'Alfred ordered me to be made'. It is known as the 'Alfred Jewel'.

When Alfred was a young boy, his mother encouraged him to read and memorise a book of Old English poetry. At the age of 40, Alfred asked a Welsh bishop called Asser to teach him to read and write **Latin**. Asser later wrote a biography of Alfred, and recorded "from his cradle, he was filled with the love of wisdom above all things".

Having learned Latin, Alfred was able to translate important books – particularly about Christianity – into Old English, helping to spread Christianity among his people. This was a remarkable achievement, and England would have to wait another 200 years before it was again ruled by a king who could read and write. Alfred also oversaw the writing of the **Anglo-Saxon Chronicle** – an enormous history book that kept a record of every important event that happened in England until 1154.

In 899, Alfred died. King Alfred's rule laid the foundation on which his descendants would build the unified Anglo-Saxon Kingdom of England. He remains the only king in English history to be remembered as 'the Great'.

Alfred and the cakes

According to a popular legend, while Alfred was hiding in the Somerset marshes, a peasant woman gave him shelter. She was unaware that he was her king, and ordered him to watch some cakes as they cooked by the fire.

Alfred had just lost his kingdom to Guthrum's Viking army, and was hiding for his life. He was so distracted trying to work out how he could defeat the Vikings and reclaim his kingdom, he allowed the cakes to burn. When the peasant woman returned, she was furious with Alfred. "You happily eat all my food, but when I give you the job of looking after it, you let it burn!" she shouted. Alfred could have told her he was the king, but he did not, and simply apologised for his mistake.

Modern illustration of Alfred and the peasant woman

Fact

Although Alfred was successful on the battlefield, he was not physically strong. He suffered from an illness throughout his life, which some historians believe was Crohn's disease. This illness often left Alfred feeling frail and depressed.

Check your understanding

1. What Anglo-Saxon kingdom did Alfred rule?
2. On what day did Guthrum's army first attack Alfred in 878?
3. What agreement did Alfred come to with Guthrum after the Battle of Edington?
4. What did Alfred do to ensure that Wessex remained safe from future Viking attacks?
5. Why did Alfred want to learn to read and write in Latin?

The Anglo-Saxon golden age

Following King Alfred's death in 899, it fell to his son King Edward the Elder to continue the fight against the Vikings.

Edward was greatly helped by his older sister, Æthelflæd, who, at the age of 15, had been sent by their father Alfred to marry the Lord of Mercia.

Æthelflæd was famed for her intelligence and strength, and with her husband she won much of Mercia back from the Vikings. When her husband died in 911, Æthelflæd continued to rule Mercia on her own as the 'Lady of Mercia', leading her army into battle. Just like her father, Æthelflæd built fortress burhs on land won back from the Vikings, in places such as Chester, Stafford, Warwick and Tamworth. King Edward was so impressed by his tough older sister that he sent his own son, Æthelstan, to be brought up by her.

Although he is not much talked about today, some historians say Æthelstan should be remembered as the first King of England. Northumbria remained as an outpost of Viking power when he became king, centred around the Viking capital of Jorvik. Æthelstan slowly asserted Anglo-Saxon power over Northumbria, and in 937 he won a great victory at the Battle of Brunanburh, against an enormous Scottish, Viking and Northumbrian army. The Anglo-Saxon chronicle recorded, "Never was there more slaughter on this island, never yet as many people killed before this with sword's edge: never according to those who tell us from books, old wisemen, since from the east Angles and Saxons came up over the broad sea." This victory confirmed Æthelstan's rule of all England.

During his reign, Æthelstan had new coins minted for his kingdom, on which he gave himself the title *Rex Anglorum*, meaning 'King of the English'. For the first time since the Roman conquest, England could be described as a single unified country.

> **Fact**
>
> Upon her death in 918, Æthelflæd left her Mercian kingdom to her daughter Ælfwynn. However, Ælfwynn's rule lasted only a few months before her uncle Edward took the kingdom for himself and probably forced her into a **convent**.

Peace and prosperity

For the next 50 years, England experienced a **golden age**: there was unprecedented peace, and people grew increasingly wealthy. Kings ruled alongside the **Witan**, a collection of Anglo-Saxon noblemen and senior members of the Church summoned by the king to offer him advice and discuss important issues. This ensured that the king's decisions had the support of the people he ruled.

Anglo-Saxon England also developed a single currency, a legal code written in Old English and a centralised government. Anglo-Saxon government sent out royal charters to every corner of the kingdom. The country was divided into individual

Anglo-Saxon silver penny from the late 10th or early 11th century

counties, known as **shires**, each ruled by an Anglo-Saxon **earl**. Shires were in turn divided into 'hundreds', which in theory covered enough land to support 100 households. The borders of some of these shires remain unchanged today as England's counties.

Return of the Vikings

In 990, Viking invaders once again began harassing England's coastline. England's king at the time was Æthelred the Unready. Unlike his predecessors, Æthelred was a poor leader and unable to unify his earls to repel the Viking invaders.

Æthelred repeatedly paid off the Viking invaders with danegeld, but it never took long before the Vikings returned asking for even larger sums of money. The year Æthelred died in 1016, England's throne passed to a Viking king named Canute (see box). This toing and froing of England's throne between Anglo-Saxon and Viking kings would only end with the arrival of a new force in northern Europe – the Normans.

King Canute

During his 19-year rule of England, King Canute (sometimes spelled Cnut) was a thoughtful and popular king. Although a Viking from Denmark, he signalled that he wanted to rule England as an English king. Most Anglo-Saxon earls were allowed to keep their land, and Canute paid off his own Viking army with one of the largest danegelds ever raised, £90 000, to ensure that they returned to Denmark and left England in peace.

Overseas, Canute's **empire** steadily grew: he gained Denmark in 1019, Norway in 1028 and some parts of Sweden. In the most famous story from his reign, a courtier who was trying to win favour with the king told Canute that he even had control of the seas.

Canute did not approve of such flattery, and demanded that his throne be taken to the seashore. Here, Canute sat and ordered the tide not to advance. The waves ignored him and drenched his feet. In response, King Canute told his courtiers: "Let the world know that the power of kings is empty and worthless compared with the majesty of God."

Modern illustration of King Canute failing to halt the advancing tide

Check your understanding

1. Why did King Edward send his son to be brought up by his aunt Æthelflæd?
2. Why was the Battle of Brunanburh such an important victory for the Anglo-Saxons?
3. What was significant about the reign of Alfred's grandson Æthelstan?
4. What role did the Witan play in the government of England?
5. What did King Canute do to win the favour of the Anglo-Saxon people he ruled?

Unit 1: Anglo-Saxon England
Knowledge organiser

731 The Venerable Bede completes *The Ecclesiastical History of the English People*

410 The Roman army leaves Britain

400–600 The Angles and Saxons arrive in England from Germany

597 Augustine arrives in England to convert the Anglo-Saxons to Christianity

793 The Vikings attack the monastery on Lindisfarne

Key vocabulary

AD Used to record historical dates as number of years after Christ's birth: Anno Domini

Anglo-Saxon Chronicle A contemporary history of England, begun during the reign of Alfred the Great

Anglo-Saxons Two Germanic tribes who invaded England from Germany, between 400 and 600 AD

Archaeologist Someone who examines objects and locations from the past, often through excavation

Archbishop of Canterbury The most senior bishop in, and leader of, the Church of England

Blood Eagle A notorious Viking method for killing their enemies

Burh A fortified town which ruled a local area

Celts The dominant population in Britain until the arrival of the Anglo-Saxons

Century A period of 100 years, often used to describe different historical periods

Convent Building housing a religious community of nuns

Danegeld Large sums of money given to Vikings to prevent further invasions

Danelaw English territory given over to Viking rule

Dark Ages A term sometimes used to describe the years that followed the fall of the Roman Empire

Earl A noble title, developed during the Anglo-Saxon period to describe the ruler of a county

Empire A group of countries or states presided over by a single ruler

Fyrd Part-time Anglo-Saxon army which could be called up to fight at times of war

Golden age A period of flourishing in the history of a nation or an art form

Great Heathen Army A large force of Viking warriors who invaded England during the 9th century

Illumination Richly decorated religious manuscript from the medieval period

Jorvik The centre of Viking power in England, on the site of modern-day York

Latin A classical language spoken by the Romans and used by the Catholic Church

Longboat A Viking ship that combined both sails and oars

Mercia Anglo-Saxon kingdom in central England, covering what is today called the Midlands

Monastery Building housing a religious community of monks

865 The invasion of the 'Great Heathen Army'

878 Alfred the Great defeats the 'Great Heathen Army' at the Battle of Edington

937 Æthelstan's victory at the Battle of Brunanburh confirms Anglo-Saxon rule of all England

899 Alfred the Great dies

871 Alfred the Great is crowned King of Wessex

1016 The Viking ruler Canute becomes King of England

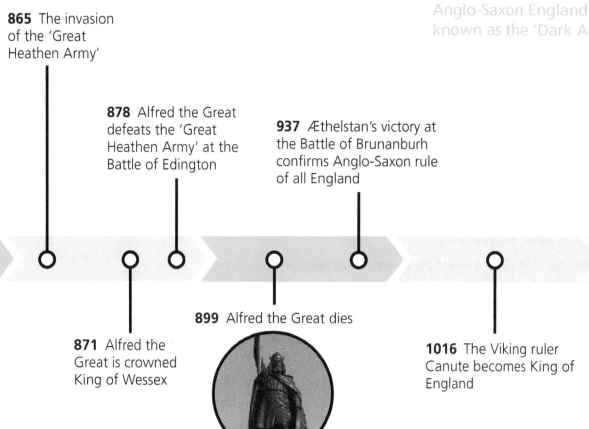

Key vocabulary

Monk A man who dedicates his entire life to God, and lives outside of normal society

Native A person born in or historically associated with a particular country or region

Pagan Someone who believes in many different gods

Shire Individual county, meaning 'area of control' in Old English

Sutton Hoo The site of an Anglo-Saxon ship burial from the 7th century AD

Valhalla The heaven for Viking warriors

Vellum A writing material made from the skin of calves, before the invention of paper

Vikings Seafaring people from Scandinavia who raided and traded across Europe, Asia and North America

Wessex Anglo-Saxon kingdom stretching across southern England

Witan A collection of Anglo-Saxon noblemen and senior clergymen who advised the king

Key people

Æthelflæd The 'lady of the Mercians' who helped expel the Vikings from England

Æthelstan Grandson of Alfred the Great, who unified England as one country

Alfred the Great The Anglo-Saxon King of Wessex who defeated the Great Heathen Army

Augustine A monk sent from Rome who converted the Anglo-Saxons to Christianity and became the first Archbishop of Canterbury

Bede An English monk who wrote the first history of England

Canute Viking King of England, who famously could not hold back the tide

Guthrum Viking king who was defeated by Alfred and given the Danelaw to rule

King Offa King of Mercia who built a 149-mile-long earthwork between England and Wales

Saxon, Norman or Viking?

In 1042, the English throne was restored to an Anglo-Saxon king named Edward the Confessor.

King Edward's rule depended upon the support of Godwin, the Earl of Wessex. Godwin was the wealthiest and most powerful nobleman in England, and his daughter Edith was married to the king. King Edward became known as 'the Confessor' because he was very religious. He focused much of his attention on building a large abbey in Westminster, ignoring his other duties as king.

On Christmas Day 1065, Edward ate an enormous feast. He took to his bed the following day feeling ill, and two weeks later on 5 January 1066 he died. Edward and Edith did not have any children, so England was thrown into confusion. Three different men claimed the English throne and each was willing to fight to the death for their claim to be king.

Harold Godwinson

Harold was the son of Godwin, the Earl of Wessex. After the death of his father, he was England's most powerful earl, and his family controlled much of the country. He was tall, good looking, an excellent fighter and popular among the Anglo-Saxon **nobles**.

Extract from the Bayeux Tapestry depicting Harold Godwinson

Harold's sister Edith was married to the king, making him Edward the Confessor's brother-in-law. However, he did not have a blood-claim to the throne. Harold claimed that on his deathbed Edward had chosen him as his successor. The day after Edward died, Harold was crowned King Harold II at Westminster Abbey. Most of the Witan were pleased to have an Anglo-Saxon as king, but some worried that Harold was simply an ambitious nobleman with no right to be king. In April 1066, a burning comet was seen in the night sky. Was it a bad **omen**, showing God's anger that England was now ruled by a king with no **royal blood**?

William, Duke of Normandy

A distant cousin of Edward the Confessor, William was one of the most feared warriors in Europe. He was born the **illegitimate** son of the Duke of Normandy and a tanner's daughter, earning him the nickname 'William the Bastard'. Despite this, he became the Duke of Normandy after his father's death in 1035. As duke, William conquered much of northern France and gained a reputation for both bravery and ruthlessness.

Extract from the Bayeux Tapestry depicting William, Duke of Normandy

William claimed that in 1051 King Edward the Confessor (who at the time had fallen out with the Godwin family) had promised him the English throne. In the spring of 1066, William was sent a banner blessed by the

Pope, showing the Pope's support for his claim to the throne. William also claimed that Harold Godwinson had sworn an **oath** of loyalty to him in 1064, and therefore supported his claim. Much confusion surrounds this event. It seems that Harold had been shipwrecked off the French coast, and was taken prisoner by William. Harold later claimed that his oath of loyalty to William was invalid, as he had only sworn it to gain his freedom.

Harald Hardrada

Harald Hardrada (meaning 'hard ruler') was a powerful Viking king of Norway, who had fought across Europe and Asia. He vowed to add England to his Scandinavian empire, claiming that England still belonged to the Vikings as it had during the days of King Canute.

Hardrada had a very useful ally: Harold Godwinson's hot-headed younger brother Tostig. Harold and Tostig had fallen out bitterly in 1065 when Harold stripped his brother of his earldom in Northumbria for being a bad ruler, and sent him into **exile**. Tostig was now willing to betray his brother and fight for Hardrada's Vikings.

Fact

Once, when the Duke of Normandy was laying siege to Alençon Castle in France, the inhabitants taunted him about his mother's lowly status. Having taken the castle, William had his revenge by cutting off the hands and feet of every inhabitant.

Battle of Stamford Bridge

In September 1066, King Harold's army was stationed in the south of England preparing for an invasion from the **Normans**. However, he received the shocking news that Hardrada and Tostig had invaded England's north-east coast and taken control of the old Viking capital, York. Harold marched his army north to meet the Vikings, covering 180 miles in just four days.

This caught the Viking army completely by surprise, and the two armies met at a location called Stamford Bridge on 25 September. Many Vikings did not even have time to put on their armour, and Harold's army destroyed them, killing both Hardrada and Tostig. Of an invasion fleet of around 300 ships, fewer than 30 ships were needed to take what remained of the Viking army back to Norway.

According to a Saxon legend, a great Viking fighter held off the English attack on the bridge, so that they could not finish off the retreating Viking army. Nobody could kill this fearsome Viking, until an English soldier had the clever idea of floating under the bridge and thrusting his spear into the Viking's foot.

Stamford Bridge in Yorkshire, the site of the battle today, where an 18th-century bridge now stands

Check your understanding

1. Why was the death of Edward the Confessor met with such confusion?
2. What was Harold Godwinson's claim to the English throne?
3. What was William of Normandy's claim to the English throne?
4. What was Harald Hardrada's claim to the English throne?
5. How did Harold Godwinson defeat Hardrada's Viking army?

The Battle of Hastings

Harold's victory at Stamford Bridge was an astonishing success. However, while Harold's army was celebrating, a messenger arrived with dreadful news from the south.

On 28 September 1066, just three days after the Battle of Stamford Bridge, William, Duke of Normandy had landed on the south-east coast of England with his invasion force.

Since August, William had been camped on the French coast ready to invade, but the winds had not been in his favour, and by the end of September it seemed he had missed his chance. Harold even called in his navy, which had been guarding the English Channel, thinking that a Norman invasion would be delayed until the following year. But all of a sudden the winds changed and William was able to sail across the Channel unchallenged.

Ruins of Battle Abbey. The abbey was built by William the Conqueror on the site of the Battle of Hastings

William's Norman army numbered 10 000 men, with 3000 heavily armoured Norman **knights** on horseback: the tanks of medieval Europe. As William stepped off his boat, he tripped and fell on the beach. His troops looked worried at this bad omen, but as he rose William picked up two fists full of sand and declared, "Look how easily I take this land!"

Harold's army marches south

The Norman army marched 10 miles inland to Hastings, where they quickly built a wooden castle, and prepared for Harold to attack. With wounds still fresh from battle, Harold's army began a 200-mile trek from Stamford Bridge to the south coast. They stopped in London, where many of Harold's advisers begged him to rest and rebuild his forces over the winter before attacking the Norman army in the spring. However, Harold wanted to surprise William just as he had surprised Hardrada's Viking army. After just one week gaining reinforcements, Harold resumed his march south.

At 9 a.m. on 14 October, the two armies met 10 miles outside Hastings. Harold had left many of his best soldiers in the north, but kept the core of his army: 3000 fearsome **huscarls** – the king's professional soldiers and bodyguard. The rest of the army consisted of the fyrd: around 5000 part-time soldiers, some armed with little more than a pike.

> ### Fact
>
> The **Bayeux Tapestry** is 70 metres long and tells the entire story of William of Normandy's **conquest** of England. It is one of medieval Europe's most important artefacts. Bishop Odo, William's half-brother, commissioned the tapestry during the 1070s as a gift to his brother.

Extract from the Bayeux Tapestry

The battle

Arriving at the battlefield, Harold's army took the high ground on top of Senlac Hill and formed a long defensive 'shield wall' of troops chanting "ut, ut!" ("out, out!").

This was an excellent start for the Saxons: the Norman knights could not break through the wall as their horses lost speed galloping uphill, and the Norman archers were ineffective when they fired their arrows upwards. Harold's army stood its ground, taking great swings at the Norman knights with their axes. At one point, a rumour spread across the battlefield that William, Duke of Normandy was dead. But then William removed his helmet and called out to his troops that he was still alive.

Modern illustration of the death of King Harold

After hours of struggling to break through the Saxon shield wall, the Normans called a retreat. Harold's army was overjoyed and broke out of their formation to chase and kill off the retreating Norman soldiers. However, the retreat had been a trick: William had ordered it to tempt the Saxon soldiers away from the high ground and to break their shield wall. The Normans now regrouped and picked off the disorganised Saxon soldiers. King Harold was killed, but to this day there is no agreement about how this happened (see box).

Without their king, most of the Saxon soldiers fled the battlefield, but Harold's huscarls – who were sworn to protect the king – fought to the death. The brutal battle lasted 6 hours and William was victorious. Having defeated Harold's army, William could spread his power throughout England. William, Duke of Normandy was now 'William the Conqueror', and the history of England had been changed forever.

The death of King Harold

There remains much disagreement among historians over how Harold died. The first account of the battle, written by the Bishop of Amiens, states that four knights were sent to find Harold on the battlefield and kill him. One knight knocked him to the floor, while two others beheaded and **disembowelled** the Saxon king.

However, in later accounts Harold was said to have been struck in the eye with an arrow, and this is what the Bayeux Tapestry appears to show beneath the words '*Harold Rex Interfectus Est*' (King Harold is killed).

Check your understanding

1. What stroke of luck did William, Duke of Normandy enjoy at the end of September?
2. Why did Harold Godwinson hurry into fighting the Norman army?
3. Who had the stronger army at the start of the Battle of Hastings: the Normans or the Saxons?
4. How did the Norman army's false retreat give them the chance to win the battle?
5. What story does the Bayeux Tapestry tell?

The Norman conquest

On Christmas Day 1066, two months after he defeated Harold, William was crowned King William I of England at Westminster Abbey.

The Norman knights guarding the coronation were fearful of a popular rebellion, and mistook cheers from inside the Abbey as a revolt. In response, they burned the surrounding houses and killed any Englishmen too slow to flee. It was a violent beginning to a violent reign.

Following his victory against King Harold at Hastings, William's approach to conquering England was brutally effective. Wherever resistance or rebellion occurred, his heavily armoured knights descended on the Anglo-Saxon communities, burning down villages and slaughtering the inhabitants. Within a few years, England's two million Anglo-Saxon inhabitants were living under the military occupation of just 20 000 Norman invaders.

Silver English penny of William the Conqueror

Norman nobles

Before invading England, William promised the Norman knights who fought for him that they would be richly rewarded with English land. The Anglo-Saxon noblemen, many of whom died on the battlefield at Hastings, had their land seized from their families and given to Norman knights. William established a **royal court** consisting of French noblemen, and a new ruling class with French names, such as Beaufort, Neville and Sinclair, spread across the country.

Wherever they were granted land, Norman nobles built large defensive structures with a French name: 'castle'. At first, these were simple **'motte-and-bailey castles'**, which were quick and easy to build: a ditch would be dug and the earth would create an artificial hill, on top of which a wooden tower would be built. Gradually, these were replaced with stronger, stone castles – stern buildings that symbolised a foreign, occupying force.

The Harrying of the North

Many Anglo-Saxons rebelled against Norman rule. In the north-east of England, the local population twice rose up against their new **lords**. On the second occasion in 1069, the northern rebels took Durham Castle, murdered its Norman earl, Robert de Commines, and slaughtered most of his garrison. The rebels then took York and proclaimed Edward the Confessor's Anglo-Saxon nephew, Edgar the Ætheling, to be the rightful King of England.

William was furious. He vowed to make an example of the northern rebels. His army marched north, and burned to the ground every village between York and Durham. Farm animals were slaughtered, crops were destroyed, and the fields were laced with salt so that no more food could be grown. Much of the population was killed, and whole areas of the north-east became uninhabited wastelands. One estimate suggests 100 000 people starved to death and, while this was probably an exaggeration, England's north-east remained sparsely populated for centuries to come.

The Harrying of the North showed William the Conqueror at his most ruthless. The Norman chronicler Orderic Vitalis wrote, "I have often praised William before, but I cannot for this act, which caused both the innocent and the guilty alike to die by slow starvation… Such brutal slaughter cannot go unpunished."

Modern illustration of the Harrying of the North

Hereward the Wake

The east of England had long been a stronghold of Anglo-Saxon power, and it was here the final rebellion against Norman rule occurred in 1070. The land surrounding a town called Ely was made up of marshes and rivers, and often covered in mist. Here, an Anglo-Saxon noble named Hereward the Wake and his band of outlaws would ambush Norman knights, kill them and disappear into the mist.

Hereward's stand against the Normans came to an end when William arrived outside Ely and built a two-mile wooden causeway across the marshes. Norman knights rode into the town, and the Saxon rebels were killed, imprisoned, blinded or had their arms chopped off. Hereward escaped, and some claimed that William had spared his life on purpose as he admired his bravery.

Hereward's heroic deeds, along with his sword known as 'Brainbiter', quickly passed into popular legend, but such stories were a small comfort for Saxons living under Norman rule.

Norman rule

Few Anglo-Saxon nobles survived William's invasion, and those that did were forced to swear an oath of loyalty to their new king. A favourite trick of William's was to demand a noble's son as a hostage, to make sure that the noble stayed loyal. At first, William suggested that he might learn English, but soon it became clear he would not. French became the language of government, business and the royal court, and England entered a new era under the rule of William and his Norman descendents.

> ### Fact
>
> After the Norman Conquest, many French words entered the English language, such as castle, battle, punishment, judge, colour and fruit.

Check your understanding

1. Why did William the Conqueror's coronation end in violence?
2. What happened to the land belonging to England's Anglo-Saxon noblemen?
3. What did William the Conqueror do to punish the rebels who rose up against him in the north-east?
4. How did William the Conqueror finally defeat Hereward the Wake?
5. What was one of the tactics William used to ensure loyalty from the Anglo-Saxon nobility?

Unit 2: Norman England
The feudal system

Under the control of William and his Norman knights, English society was transformed and a rigid social structure developed.

The higher up you were, the more land, wealth and power you held. The lower down you were, the poorer and less free you became.

English society had a clear **hierarchy**, shaped like a pyramid: the few at the top were the strongest, and the many at the bottom were the weakest, owing their duty and service to those above them. Anyone below you was your '**vassal**', and anyone above you was your 'lord'. This social structure was called the **feudal system**.

The king

Right at the top of the feudal system was the king. It was believed that the king was appointed by God, and only those with royal blood, who were descended from William the Conqueror, could sit on the throne. The king was answerable only to God, and all who lived in his kingdom were his **subjects**. However, the king still needed loyal friends to rule different parts of his kingdom on his behalf.

The barons

As the king needed loyal friends, he granted land to his **barons**: around 200 of the most powerful knights in the country. In return for their land, the king's barons had to pay **homage** to him and swear an oath of **fealty**. This meant that if ever there was a war, the barons had to fight on behalf of their king. In the centre of their vast stretches of land, barons built fortified castles to keep them safe from enemy attacks. Some had the noble title of 'Earl', and their titles and lands were **hereditary**, meaning that they passed down from the father to his eldest son.

Illustration of King William I

At the same level of power as the barons were the **bishops** and archbishops of the medieval Church. The Church was extremely powerful, and owned much of England's land. Its bishops enjoyed huge wealth and influence and were part of the ruling class.

The knights

In order to fight for their king, barons needed their own armies. So they divided their own land into smaller areas led by their knights. Each baron had around 20 knights. A knight would swear an oath of fealty to his baron, and gain a number of manor houses or smaller castles in return.

The peasants

Below the knights were the **peasants**, who made up the great majority of medieval society. Many were bound to work the land of their lord until the day they died. Some peasants were not allowed to marry or leave

Illustration of a Norman knight

home without their lord's permission. A lord would grant his peasants a small area of land to farm, and they had to work his land in return. The difference between a kind and a cruel lord could mean the difference between happiness and misery for a medieval vassal.

The Domesday Book

Two years before he died, William the Conqueror ordered that a survey should be written detailing the possessions of every single settlement in England. As king, William wanted to know precisely what this new country of his contained. Once he knew what the English people owned, he could tax them accordingly to pay for his armies and castles.

For two years, Norman commissioners were sent the length and breadth of England, with the order that not a single cow nor pig should escape their notice. They visited 13 418 different towns and villages, and wrote down two million words. The official name of the record was 'The King's Roll', but it became more commonly known as the '**Domesday Book**'.

'Doomsday' is another name for the Day of Judgment, when Christians believe that Jesus Christ will return to the Earth and pass judgment on both the living and the dead. The Anglo-Saxons chose this nickname with a sarcastic sense of humour, as they disliked a foreign king forcing them to declare everything they owned so that he could pass judgment on them.

Today, the Domesday Book provides us with a fascinating picture of what England was like at the end of the 11th century, right down to the last fishpond and beehive. We hear the nicknames of English peasants, such as Alwin the Rat and Ralph the Haunted. In 1085, Birmingham, which is England's second largest city today, was a small village with just nine families and two ploughs.

Modern illustration of the writing of the Domesday book

Fact

Anglo-Saxon women whose husbands or fathers died at the Battle of Hastings had little choice but to marry one of William's knights in order to retain their lands. Others fled to convents to avoid such a fate. Of the 1400 landowners mentioned in the Domesday Book in 1086, only 20 are female.

Fact

Over 70 English forests became Royal hunting grounds. If a peasant was found hunting there, he could be punished by blinding or mutilation. Some peasants were even made to wear deer skin and be hunted themselves!

Check your understanding

1. What was the shape of medieval English society?
2. In return for being granted land, what did barons do for the king?
3. What powers did a medieval lord have over the peasants who worked his land?
4. Why did William the Conqueror commission the Domesday Book to be written?
5. How did the Domesday Book earn its nickname?

The Norman monarchs

Towards the end of his life, William the Conqueror grew very fat, but this did not stop him from going on military campaigns.

In 1087, while laying siege to the town of Mantes in northern France, William's horse stood on some hot stones and reared up. The king was impaled on the pommel of his saddle and he died 6 weeks later.

As seemed to be the tradition for Norman kings, William did not get on well with each of his three sons. He ruled an empire stretching across England and Normandy and, by right, all his land should have passed to his eldest son Robert. However, William disliked Robert – he even nicknamed him 'Curthose' or 'stubby legs'. So, William gave Normandy to his eldest son Robert, England to his middle son William, and £5000 to his youngest son Henry. This would prove to be a grave mistake.

William, Robert and Henry I

William II was an unpleasant **monarch**. Nicknamed 'Rufus' for his red hair, he was angry and short-tempered, and offended the Church through his open disdain for religion. On a summer's day in August 1100, William was hunting in the New Forest with his close friend Walter Tirel. Tirel was known for being a good archer, but when shooting at a stag he missed and hit William II straight in the chest. The king dropped to the floor and died instantly. Tirel fled the scene, travelling to France where he died later that year in exile.

William's younger brother Henry, who was also at the hunt, acted quickly. On hearing the news of his brother's death he rode to Winchester and three days later was crowned Henry I. For centuries, historians have wondered whether the death of William II was an accident or a deliberate plot.

In 1106, Henry I captured his eldest brother Robert on the battlefield in Normandy. He seized Robert's French lands and imprisoned him in Cardiff Castle for the last 30 years of his life. Through imprisoning one older brother and (perhaps) killing another, in just six years the youngest son of William the Conqueror had gone from ruling nothing to ruling over the whole of his father's empire. Henry I ruled England for 35 peaceful years.

Henry I married a princess named Matilda, who was descended from the Anglo-Saxon House of Wessex. Together, they had one son named William, but he died on board the *White Ship* in 1120 (see box).

> ### Fact
> Having grown fat in his old age, William was too large for his stone coffin at his funeral. When the attendants tried to force his body inside the coffin his body burst. The mourners fled as a putrid smell spread through the church.

Modern illustration of the sinking of the *White Ship*

The *White Ship*

On a cold November evening, Henry I and his 17-year-old son William were due to sail for England from the Norman port of Barfleur. Henry I left early, but William and his friends chose to stay behind getting drunk and finally left around midnight. The young men were on a newly built vessel named the *White Ship*, and they challenged their crew to overtake the king's ship.

The *White Ship's* crew had also been drinking. As the vessel left the port, it struck a rock off the Normandy coast. The boat sank, killing Henry I's only son and **heir**, along with many other **Anglo-Norman** nobles.

The Anarchy

With Henry I's only son dead, attention turned to his daughter Matilda. After being forced to marry a German emperor at 11 years old, Matilda had been living in Europe. In both 1126 and 1131, Henry made his barons swear an oath of allegiance to Matilda as his heir. However, when Henry died in 1135, while Matilda was pregnant with her third son in France, her cousin Stephen seized the throne. The Church and most nobles switched their support, but Matilda went to war to regain her rightful crown. This plunged England into a 19-year **civil war**. Great areas of the country had no royal authority, leaving the people at the mercy of cruel barons who used the civil war as an excuse to terrorise their vassals; a period remembered as 'The **Anarchy**'.

Although Matilda successfully captured Stephen in 1141, she retreated to Normandy, disheartened by the death of some key supporters. However, her son Henry was proclaimed Stephen's heir, and when he became King Henry II in 1154, Matilda ruled over England's often-disputed territories successfully for over a decade.

14th-century illustration of Empress Matilda

Fact

The Anglo-Saxon Chronicle gives a vivid account of 'The Anarchy', describing people being forced into labour, imprisoned and tortured: "the lands were all laid waste by such deeds; and men said openly that Christ and his saints were asleep."

Check your understanding

1. How did William the Conqueror split his empire between his three sons when he died?
2. What were the suspicious circumstances surrounding William II's death?
3. Which of William the Conqueror's three sons eventually ended up ruling England?
4. Why did the sinking of the *White Ship* in 1120 throw England into a state of confusion?
5. Why was the civil war between Stephen and Matilda so unpleasant for the English population?

Knowledge organiser

1051 Edward the Confessor promises the English throne to William, Duke of Normandy

1064 Harold Godwinson swears an oath of loyalty to William, Duke of Normandy

1066 (Sep) The Battle of Stamford Bridge

1066 (Oct) The Battle of Hastings

1066 (Dec) William I crowned King of England

Key vocabulary

Anarchy A state of disorder caused by a lack of law or authority

Anglo-Norman The ruling class in England after 1066, composed of Normans who had settled in England

Baron The highest rank of medieval society, ruling land directly on behalf of the king

Bayeux Tapestry A 70-metre long embroidered cloth depicting William of Normandy's conquest of England

Bishop A Christian clergyman with authority over a large number of priests and churches

Civil war A war between two sides from the same nation

Conquest Taking control of a place or people through military force

Disembowel To cut someone open and remove their internal organs

Domesday Book A book commissioned by William the Conqueror detailing the possessions of every settlement in England

Exile Being forced to live outside your native country, typically for political reasons

Fealty A pledge of loyalty from a feudal vassal to their lord

Feudal system The structure of medieval society, where land was exchanged for service and loyalty

Heir A person set to inherit property or a title, often used to mean next in line to the throne

Hereditary Passed through a family, from parents to their children

Hierarchy A form of social organisation where people are ranked according to status or power

Homage The practice of giving an annual payment to your Lord to show that you are their vassal

Huscarls The professional bodyguard of Anglo-Saxon kings

Illegitimate Not recognised as lawful; once used to describe someone born of unmarried parents

Knights Soldiers on horseback who belonged to the nobility

Lord A general term for a medieval landholder, or a member of the peerage today

Monarch A royal head of state; can be a king, queen or emperor

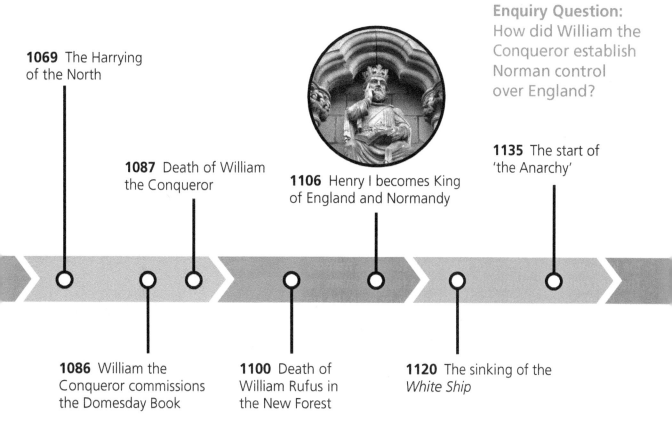

1069 The Harrying of the North

1087 Death of William the Conqueror

1106 Henry I becomes King of England and Normandy

1135 The start of 'the Anarchy'

1086 William the Conqueror commissions the Domesday Book

1100 Death of William Rufus in the New Forest

1120 The sinking of the *White Ship*

Key vocabulary

Motte-and-bailey castle A simple fortification with an artificial hill and a defensive courtyard

Noble Member of the nobility, with land and titles that pass through the generations

Normans People from a region in northern France, who were descended from Viking invaders

Oath A solemn promise, often said to be witnessed by God

Omen An event that is thought to foretell the future, perhaps as a message from God

Peasant The lowest member of medieval society, usually a farm labourer

Royal blood Those who are blood relatives of a ruling monarch

Royal court A collection of nobles and clergymen, known as courtiers, who advise the monarch

Subject A member of a country or territory under the rule of a monarch

Vassal Anyone who was below you in medieval society, and had to call you 'my lord'

Key people

Edward the Confessor Anglo-Saxon King of England whose death triggered the Norman invasion

Empress Matilda The daughter of Henry I, who fought for the English throne during 'The Anarchy'

Harald Hardrada A fierce Viking warrior, who made a claim for the English throne in 1066

Harold Godwinson The last Anglo-Saxon King of England, who led the Saxons at the Battle of Hastings

Henry I The youngest son of William the Conqueror, who became king after the death of his brother William II

Hereward the Wake A legendary Saxon rebel, who held out against the Norman invaders in Ely

William, Duke of Normandy A French duke who conquered England in 1066

William II The middle son of William the Conqueror, who was nicknamed 'Rufus' due to his red hair

The medieval village

Today, the proportion of England's population who farm the land is 1 per cent. During the medieval period, 90 per cent of the population worked the land.

Life for a medieval peasant was tough: the average age of death was 30 years old, and 40 was considered to be old. Peasants lived in a village, normally with around 25 households. The ultimate authority within a village was the lord, and at the centre of the village stood his **manor**. The lord could be anyone high up in the feudal system, such as a knight, the Archbishop of Canterbury, or even the king. Some lords owned multiple manors so a **steward** would look after the manor on his behalf.

Farming the land

The manor was surrounded by fields, which were then divided into long thin strips, wide enough for an ox to pull a plough up one side and down the other. This was known as **strip farming**. The lord gave each peasant a number of strips to farm for themselves, but in return they had to spend around three days each week farming the lord's land, known as the **demesne**.

Peasants had to pay all sorts of different taxes to their lord, such as the wood-penny, the foddercorn and the bodel silver. One tax, called the heriot, stated that when a peasant died they had to give their best animal to the lord. In addition, one-tenth of all of their farm produce had to be given to the Church each year, a payment called the **tithe**.

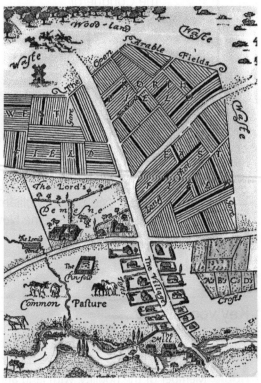

Map of a medieval village

The peasant's life moved with the seasons. In the early spring, land was ploughed with an ox to turn over the earth, providing fresh soil for crops. In this soil, the peasant sowed their seeds. By late summer, the crops were ready to harvest. The villagers would wait for a few days of sunny weather to dry the crops, before harvesting them as quickly as possible. All other jobs stopped during the harvest and the whole village – men, women and children – took part. They reaped the crops with a large blade called a 'scythe' and bundled them into 'sheaves'. Peasants also had to harvest the lord's fields, something known as 'boon-time'.

Through the autumn, the crops were threshed to separate the edible seed from the chaff (husks). The seed could then be cooked or ground to make flour for bread. Every year, peasants would struggle to harvest enough food to feed themselves until the next spring. If they suffered a bad harvest, they would simply starve.

Today, it is hard for us to imagine the conditions in which peasants lived. The poorest peasant families inhabited one small, single-room hut. This was made out of wood and straw, with walls made from **wattle and daub**. The family all slept together on one straw mattress. The huts had no windows and a hole in the ceiling instead of a chimney, so the smoke from the fire filled the room. Farm animals such as cows and sheep would also be kept in the hut to provide heat during the winter. Imagine the smell!

Outside the hut, peasants kept a small plot of land, known as a **croft**, where they grew vegetables, and kept bees, chickens, geese and sheep. Breakfast would usually consist of bread and weak beer, and lunch would be the same, perhaps with some cheese. Beer was drunk throughout the day by adults and children, as water was often too dirty to drink. For their main meal, peasants ate a stew of vegetables and grains called '**pottage**'. Meat would rarely be eaten, because animals were too valuable as a source of milk, eggs and textiles.

The one building made of durable stone, aside from the manor, would normally be the church. As they were built of stone, many medieval churches still stand at the centre of English villages today. Around 20 days a year were religious holy days, or 'holidays'. Sometimes not much religious worship would actually take place. On holy days, the lord of the manor would provide a feast and entertainments, and the whole village celebrated together. If the peasants were lucky, the lord would provide meat and ale.

Illustration from a medieval manuscript showing a lazy ploughman (top right) and a hard working peasant sowing seeds (bottom right)

There were some other jobs available to peasants aside from farming. Peasants could appoint a reeve, who represented them in discussions with the lord. The constable was in charge of arresting criminals and organising the law courts, and the miller ran the lord's flourmill. The names of these jobs, along with other medieval jobs such as Smith, Fowler, Cooper and Haywood, remain common surnames today.

Fact

The measurement of an 'acre' originally meant the area of land that one ox could plough in a day.

Check your understanding

1. How did the proportion of people in medieval England who farmed the land differ from today?

2. What did peasants have to do in return for being given strips of land by their lord?

3. When would medieval peasants harvest their crops?

4. Why did peasants keep live farm animals inside their homes?

5. What would usually happen during a medieval holy day?

The medieval castle

Medieval England was often in a state of war. Kings fought other kings. Barons fought other barons. Sometimes, barons would unite and fight their own king.

Due to this instability, English kings and barons needed strong, well-defended castles in which their families and armies could seek protection. The castle was the ultimate symbol of power in the medieval world.

At first, these were simple motte-and-bailey castles, which were easy to build. A ditch would be dug, and the soil from the ground would be used to create an artificial hill called a 'motte'. On top of this motte a wooden tower would be built. Beneath the motte would be a small courtyard called a 'bailey'. When the castle was attacked, the inhabitants of the bailey could seek shelter in the tower. Motte-and-bailey castles were quick and cheap to build. However, the wood would soon begin to rot, and could easily be burned down. So, the early wooden castles were replaced with larger, stronger stone castles.

Clifford's Tower in York. Built on the orders of William the Conqueror, it sits upon a Norman motte.

Defending a castle

The chief aim of castle design was to make it impossible for enemies to enter. During the medieval period, a number of clever ideas were developed to improve a castle's defences.

- **Curtain walls:** This was an outer wall around the castle, often up to 12 metres thick.

- **Moat:** A **moat** was a ditch dug to prevent attackers and their **siege** weapons from reaching the wall.

- **Gatehouse:** The gateway to enter the castle was a weak point for attack, so it would be heavily defended, often with its own towers on either side.

- **Murderholes:** These were gaps in the roof of the gatehouse through which invading soldiers could be pelted with stones, waste materials and boiling water.

- **Drawbridge:** This was a bridge from the gatehouse over the moat. It could be lifted up when the castle was attacked.

- **Arrow slits:** These long, thin windows were just wide enough to fire an arrow out of, but not large enough to climb through.

- **Crenellations:** These regular gaps running along the top of a castle wall, like teeth, allowed defenders to fire arrows at attackers but quickly take cover again.

- **Keep:** This large stone building at the heart of the castle had enormous thick walls and small slit windows. The **keep** was strongly defended, and the last refuge for the castle's inhabitants if the walls were **breached**.

> ### Fact
>
> During the reign of King John, Lincoln Castle was controlled by Nicola de la Haye. She inherited the castle from her father, and famously defended it against two sieges. King John recognised her bravery and appointed her Sheriff of Lincolnshire in 1216.

Whittington Castle in Shropshire, England

Attacking a castle

Each new technology developed for defending castles would be matched by a new technology developed for attack. For attackers, the main aim was to create a hole in the castle wall, called a breach, through which their army could enter.

- **Mangonel:** This large catapult used twisted animal hair as an elasticised spring to fire rocks at the castle walls.

- **Trebuchet:** This was a more advanced catapult, which used a counterweight and sling, and could hurl large rocks great distances with a strong force – perfect for creating a breach.

- **Battering ram:** Made from a large tree trunk and given a metal tip, this was used to batter down castle doors. It was sometimes hung from a frame on wheels and covered with a roof for protection.

- **Siege tower:** Also known as a belfry, a **siege tower** was a large wooden tower with ladders inside that could be wheeled up to a castle wall and used to climb up and over.

- **Undermining:** **Undermining** involved digging a tunnel beneath a castle wall and lighting a fire. The fire would cause the tunnel to collapse and the castle walls to fall in, creating a breach.

- **Siege:** If all else failed, an army would simply surround a castle allowing nobody to come in or out. The inhabitants would slowly starve until they surrendered – or died.

Developments in castle building

Castle designs kept on improving. Missiles from catapults could knock a hole in flat walls but would glance off curved walls, so round towers were developed. During the Crusades, returning European knights built '**concentric castles**', based on those they had seen in Byzantium and the Islamic world. Concentric castles had two or more curtain walls, which meant archers defending the inner curtain wall could fire at the enemy army as they attacked the outer curtain wall.

Castle technology became highly advanced during the medieval period. However, the original defensive function of castles began to fade over the centuries. Noblemen became more concerned with living in houses that were comfortable and visually appealing, rather than well defended.

The role of castles was finally ended by the arrival of a new invention from China: gunpowder. With this new technology, cannons could be used to blow apart a castle's stone defences. By the 15th century, the medieval castle was becoming obsolete.

Modern illustration of a trebuchet

Fact

Trebuchets also hurled rotting animals that could spread disease into castles. If an inhabitant from the castle was captured trying to escape, a trebuchet might even be used to hurl them back inside!

Aerial view of a concentric castle

Check your understanding

1. What were the advantages and disadvantages of a motte-and-bailey castle?
2. What was the chief aim of a castle's design?
3. What was the main aim for an army attacking a castle?
4. How would a siege ensure that an enemy army could eventually take a castle?
5. Where did European knights learn about the technology for concentric castles?

The medieval knight

Medieval England was ruled by a warrior class of knights. These were heavily armed fighters on horseback, whose fearsome cavalry charges at a standing enemy could win or lose a battle. The number of knights in England peaked during the reign of Henry II, who had around 6000 at his service.

Becoming a knight

At the age of seven, boys of noble birth were sent to live with another noble family, perhaps an uncle or close friend. Here, they served in the lord's household as a page. In return, a page would be trained in activities such as horse riding, sword fighting and the rules of 'courtly' manners, known as **chivalry** (see box).

Having reached the age of 14, a page moved on to being a **squire**. A squire was a personal servant to a knight: the word comes from the French word '*écuyer*' meaning 'shield-holder'. The squire followed his knight into battle, and performed essential tasks such as preparing his food, readying his horse, and – most importantly – helping him put on his suit of **armour**.

Reenactment of a medieval **jousting** tournament

In return, the squire received intensive training. This involved physical exercise to prepare him for the battlefield, such as wrestling, weight lifting, sword fighting and acrobatics. It also included learning chivalric behaviour, such as talking politely to a noble lady or dining at a feast. If the squire fulfilled all of his tasks, he became a knight at around the age of 21.

Becoming a knight involved a ceremony called 'dubbing'. The squire knelt on one knee in front of his lord, who tapped him on the shoulder with the flat of his sword. He would then arise a knight. Some knights went through longer ceremonies, intended to symbolise different chivalric virtues.

Armour and fighting

After such intense preparation, knights were highly valued on the battlefield. No expense was spared in ensuring a knight's armour kept him alive, and suits of armour became increasingly intricate and complex. By the fourteenth century, it could take up to an hour for a squire to dress his knight for battle. First, he put on his aketon, a leather-padded garment filled with feathers to cushion blows. Then, he put on a long **chain-mail** coat, which provided protection for the upper body. After that, he put on the suit of armour, a heavy suit made from overlapping sheets of metal. Lastly, he put on the colourful surcoat, and fastened it with a leather belt.

> **Fact**
>
> One dubbing ceremony involved taking a bath to wash away sin then wearing a purple cloak to symbolise blood, black stockings to symbolise death, and a white belt to symbolise purity.

The suit of armour had to be extremely well designed to provide both complete coverage and freedom of movement. It included many rivets, pivots and hinges, which had to be regularly greased by the squire so that they did not become stiff. The glove, known as the **gauntlet**, was particularly complicated, with small individual plates allowing each finger to move freely.

The knight went into battle armed with a long **lance** to use in a **cavalry** charge. Having dropped his lance, the knight fought with a sword, a mace (a heavy club with a spiked metal head), a two-handed axe or a poleaxe (battleaxe). It was very difficult to kill a knight on the battlefield, but not impossible. Archers were effective, and the 'bodkin' arrowhead was designed to pierce armour. In addition, short stabbing swords could be thrust through the gaps in a suit of armour.

Modern illustration of a Knight's suit of armour

Chivalry

The ideal medieval knight combined brave fighting on the battlefield with 'courtly manners' off it. This code of behaviour became known as chivalry, from the French word '*chevalier*' meaning horseman.

Knights would have to swear an oath of chivalry, promising to be brave, truthful, godly, gentle, faithful and fearless. In particular, knights were expected to defend the honour of women and children. One act of chivalry was to demand a **duel** with a knight who had offended your honour. This could be done by throwing your armoured glove on the floor, an act known as 'throwing down the gauntlet'.

Heraldic crests

It was very difficult to identify a knight in a full suit of armour on the battlefield. For this reason, colourful 'surcoats' were developed. The surcoat was decorated with a **heraldic crest**, which could also be found on their shield and horse. On a heraldic crest, different colours and objects had all sorts of different meanings.

This system was known as 'heraldry'. It became so complicated that professional 'heralds' were employed to tell the difference between crests.

Check your understanding

1. What jobs did a squire perform for a knight?
2. What was the final stage that a squire went through before becoming a knight?
3. What weapons could be used to penetrate a knight's suit of armour?
4. What sort of values and behaviour were encouraged by the idea of chivalry?
5. For what purpose were heraldic crests first developed?

The medieval Church

Almost every person in medieval England was a Christian. Some people were more religious than others, but everyone believed in God, the Bible, heaven and hell.

The head of the Christian Church was the **Pope**, who was believed to be God's representative on Earth. The Pope normally lived in Rome, but his power spread across Western Europe. He could start wars, appoint churchmen in foreign countries, and even end a king's reign through expelling him from the Christian Church.

Some members of the **clergy** claimed that they only had to answer to the authority of the Pope, and were therefore independent of the king's power. Clergymen could be tried in their own church courts, which gave more lenient sentences – something known as '**Benefit of Clergy**'. Medieval kings such as Henry II and John I had fierce power struggles with the Pope over this matter.

Power of the Church

It is hard to overstate the importance of the Church in medieval English society. In many ways the Church *was* medieval society. It owned one-third of the land, and through its monasteries and abbeys provided education, hospitals, theatrical performances, historical records and welfare for the poor.

Monasteries and abbeys were religious houses in which monks and **nuns** lived and worked. In these religious houses, monks and nuns were meant to escape the corruption of the outside world and lead lives of perfect holiness. There were many different religious orders for monks, such as the Benedictines who cared for the ill and were renowned for their learning; and the Carthusians who lived solitary lives of fasting and prayer.

Some women were forced into convents by their families if a suitable marriage match could not be found. Others entered convents willingly, as they were one of the few places in the medieval world where women could gain an education or escape the perils of childbirth and forced marriage.

Religious houses boomed during the medieval period. In 1066, there were around 50 monasteries and nunneries in England, but by 1300 there were 900, housing around 17 500 monks and nuns. These buildings were like small towns, with monks and nuns working in farms and workshops, and providing shelter and services for the outside community. Some monasteries were more beautiful and more richly decorated than royal palaces, but they were all destroyed during the 1500s. Today, all we can see are their ruins. However, we can visit medieval **cathedrals**, of which 17 still stand.

> ### Fact
>
> Monks were easy to recognise. They wore a plain woollen robe called a 'habit', and had a distinctive haircut called a '**tonsure**', which was supposed to represent Christ's crown of thorns.

Modern illustration of a monk writing pages of the Bible by hand

In every medieval village, the parish church was at the centre of community life. It held church services but also acted as a hall for feasts, plays and entertainment during religious holy days.

Popular religion

Most people who lived during the medieval period could not read, so popular religion was vivid, dramatic and colourful. The Mass was performed in Latin, and would have sounded like a mysterious chant to a peasant. However, they could learn about Christianity through stained glass windows and wall paintings in churches and cathedrals.

For those who sinned on Earth, suffering of unspeakable cruelty awaited them in **purgatory** and hell. Paintings in churches, known as '**Doom Paintings**', showed what would happen in grim detail: the devil and his demons torture sinners, who are skinned, eaten, burned, boiled alive, placed in chains and poked with spikes.

Medieval Christianity was rich in ceremony and ritual. Religious holidays, such as Easter or All Hallows' Eve, each had their own traditions. These could include processions, fasting, performances of Bible stories or strange rituals such as 'creeping to the cross'.

Fact

When the tower of Lincoln Cathedral was completed in 1300, it was the tallest building in the world – taller even than the Great Pyramid in Egypt.

Pilgrimage

A **pilgrimage** was a journey to a place of religious significance. The most important pilgrimage location in England was the tomb of Thomas Becket in Canterbury, but wealthier pilgrims would travel to locations abroad, such as Rome or Jerusalem.

These journeys, especially overseas, were very dangerous and could take years to complete. Pilgrims had to travel in big groups to avoid being attacked and pack large amounts of supplies to survive the journey. Some pilgrims undertook these journeys to gain forgiveness for their sins, while others hoped to have a disease or disability cured; some just wanted to gain good fortune in life. At pilgrimage sites, '**relics**' containing body parts of saints could be prayed to, as they were believed to have miraculous powers.

The Canterbury pilgrims

The most famous English medieval poem, *The Canterbury Tales* by Geoffrey Chaucer, tells the story of around 20 pilgrims travelling from Southwark to Canterbury. The pilgrims are of all sorts: rich, poor, religious, sinful, male and female.

Check your understanding

1. What powers did the medieval Pope have?
2. What services did monasteries and abbeys provide for their local community?
3. Why did popular religion need to be so vivid, dramatic and colourful during the medieval period?
4. What fate did medieval people believe awaited those who sinned on Earth?
5. Why did the people of medieval England go on pilgrimage?

Crime and punishment

The punishment of criminals in medieval England closely followed the structure of feudal society.

If a peasant committed a petty crime such as theft, drunkenness or brawling, they were tried by their lord in a local manorial court. No lawyers were used, and cases normally took around 15 minutes. Crimes committed by more important vassals, such as knights, were tried by their local baron in a 'court of honour'.

Medieval law and order functioned without a police force. Sometimes, a village would appoint a part-time constable to make arrests, break up fights and keep the keys to the **stocks**. However, most people lived in small villages where everyone knew each other, so normally the community could police itself.

Trial by ordeal

If it could not be decided whether the defendant was innocent or guilty in a medieval trial, he or she could submit to '**trial by ordeal**'. An ordeal was a painful test, where it was believed that God would decide the verdict.

In trial by boiling water the defendant plunged his or her arm into a pan of boiling water to retrieve a stone. The arm was then wrapped in bandages, and inspected a week later. If the wound had healed, it was believed that God must have intervened to prove the defendant's innocence. If the wound had festered, the defendant was guilty. Similarly, trial by hot iron involved holding a burning hot iron in your hands and walking a short distance. Trial by water was particularly horrible. The defendant would be thrown in a village pond: if the person floated, then it was believed the water 'rejected' them, making them guilty. If the person sank, then they were innocent – but by then they were probably dead from drowning anyway!

Modern illustration of trial by boiling water

Punishments

If a defendant was found guilty, a diverse range of imaginatively cruel punishments awaited. Execution was given for significant crimes: rape, murder, or theft worth over a shilling. Lesser crimes were still brutally punished:

- **Mutilation:** This involved cutting off a body part. Often, the part was one relevant to the crime. A thief could have his hand cut off, and someone who spread false rumours might lose an ear.

- **Branding:** This was the burning of a criminal's skin with hot iron to form a permanent scar. The burn could be a particular shape, such as an 'M' for 'Malefactor', meaning evildoer.

- **Stocks:** Petty criminals were often placed in the stocks: wooden boards that locked a criminal in place by their feet or by their arms. Stocks were normally placed in a town square, so townspeople could taunt and throw rotten food at the criminal.

- **Ducking stool:** This was a wooden chair attached to a lever, used to submerge a criminal under water. The **ducking stool** was often used to punish women for adultery, prostitution or arguing with their family and neighbours (a crime known as 'scolding').

These punishments were all designed to humiliate the criminal and give them a sense of shame. The punishments were often performed in front of a crowd, ensuring that other people were discouraged from committing the same crimes.

Old stocks in Eyam village, England

Henry II and Common Law

Medieval courts were inconsistent in the punishments they gave and could often make wrong judgments. However, this situation began to change during the reign of Henry II, who reformed the English legal system during his reign from 1154 to 1189.

Henry introduced the concept of **trial by jury**, where 12 people who did not know the defendant were selected to decide upon their guilt. This practice is still fundamental to the English and United States legal systems today. In addition, Henry appointed judges to travel the country, administering the 'King's law' for important cases. The King's law tended to be fairer and more consistent than the decision of a baron or lord. In addition, the Pope outlawed trial by ordeal in 1215.

Through these measures, the concept of English **Common Law** emerged during the reign of Henry II: this was the expectation that penalties for particular crimes should be 'common' throughout the country, to achieve fairness and consistency.

Modern illustration of a manorial court

Avoiding punishment

If you were clever, you could find ways to avoid punishment in medieval England. In some monasteries it was impossible to make an arrest, so a criminal could take refuge there and remain safe for life. A criminal could also demonstrate they were a churchman by reciting Psalm 51 by heart in Latin. This would allow them to receive a more lenient sentence in a Church court through the Benefit of Clergy.

> ### Check your understanding
> 1. Where would a peasant be tried if they had committed a crime?
> 2. During trial by ordeal, who was believed to reveal the guilt or innocence of the accused?
> 3. Why were punishments such as the stocks or the ducking stool carried out in public?
> 4. Which king reformed the English legal system and introduced trial by jury?
> 5. What is meant by 'English Common Law'?

Knowledge organiser

Key vocabulary

Armour Metal covering worn by knights to protect themselves in battle

Benefit of Clergy The privilege enjoyed by clergymen to be tried in Church courts

Breach A gap in a wall or line of defence, made by an attacking army

Cathedral A large and impressive church that contains the seat of a bishop

Cavalry Soldiers mounted on horseback

Chain-mail A form of armour consisting of small interlocking metal rings

Chivalry A code of behaviour for medieval knights, emphasising bravery and good manners

Clergy Officials of the Christian Church, ordained to lead church services

Common Law The expectation that penalties for crimes should be 'common' throughout the country

Concentric castle A castle with rings of two or more curtain walls

Crenellations Gaps running along the top of the wall of a medieval castle

Croft An area of land surrounding a peasant's dwelling, used to grow crops or keep livestock

Demesne Land kept by a lord, which peasants were obliged to farm on his behalf

Doom Painting A painting showing people being sent to heaven or hell on the Day of Judgment

Duel A fight, often to the death, between two people that is used to settle an argument

Ducking stool A wooden chair attached to a lever, used to submerge a criminal under water

Gauntlet An armoured glove, and the origin of the saying 'throwing down the gauntlet'

Heraldic crest A symbol or design to show the identity of a knight on the battlefield

Jousting Medieval sport, fought by two mounted knights charging at each other armed with lances

Keep A large stone building at the heart of a medieval castle

Lance Wooden steel-tipped pole held by a horse rider while charging

Manor The house at the centre of a medieval lord's lands

Moat A ditch dug to prevent attackers from reaching the wall of a castle

Nun A woman who dedicates her entire life to God, and lives outside of normal society

Pilgrimage A religious journey, typically taken to a shrine or a site of religious importance

Pope Leader of the Catholic Church, who lives in Rome and is believed to be God's representative on Earth

Pottage A stew of vegetables and grains, eaten by peasants for their main meal

Purgatory A stage before heaven, where the dead are purged of any remaining sins

Relic An object of religious significance, often the physical or personal remains of a saint

Siege Surrounding an enemy castle allowing nobody to go in or come out

Siege tower A large wooden tower used by attackers to climb up and over castle walls

Squire The personal servant to a knight, normally aged between 14 and 21 years

Steward Servant who looked after the lord's manor on his behalf

Stocks A punishment for petty criminals, where wooden boards locked a criminal in place

Strip farming The division of large fields into many narrow strips worked by different peasants

Tithe A medieval tax, paying one-tenth of all farm produce to the Church

Tonsure The hairstyle of a medieval monk, supposed to represent Christ's crown of thorns

Trebuchet An advanced form of catapult, using a counterweight and a sling

Trial by jury A trial where 12 people consider the evidence and decide on the verdict

Illustration of peasants sowing their crop, from early 15th century France

Key vocabulary

Trial by ordeal A trial according to a painful test, where the will of God was believed to decide the verdict

Undermining Digging beneath a castle wall then lighting a fire, which causes the walls to fall in

Wattle and daub Woven sticks, covered in a mixture of mud, clay, animal dung and horsehair

Key people

Geoffrey Chaucer The greatest English poet of the medieval period, and author of the *Canterbury Tales*

Unit 4: Medieval kingship
Henry II (1154–89)

Henry II was short and stout, with freckles and red hair. He had a fiery temper, enormous reserves of energy, and a fierce personality that was both his making and his downfall.

Henry II's mother was the Empress Matilda, who had fought Stephen I for the English throne during the Anarchy (see Unit 2, Chapter 5). Towards the end of this civil war, Matilda had agreed to allow Stephen to rule, provided her son Henry succeed Stephen as king. So, in 1154, Henry was crowned king. After 19 years of brutal war, Henry II was determined to restore peace and order to the battered Kingdom of England.

As well as ruling England and Normandy, Henry II gained Anjou through his father, the Count of Anjou, and **Aquitaine** through his marriage to Eleanor of Aquitaine, a remarkably powerful queen (see Chapter 5, this unit). Henry II was a great fighter on the battlefield, and expanded his kingdom even further. He conquered Brittany, and won back land lost to Scotland and Wales during the reign of King Stephen. Henry's territory was known as the '**Angevin Empire**'. It stretched from the border with Scotland in the north to the Pyrenees in the south of France.

17th-century depiction of King Henry II

The murder of Thomas Becket

Thomas Becket was a clever young lawyer, whom Henry II made Lord Chancellor in 1155. Henry and Becket became great friends, and they enjoyed hunting and drinking together. Henry even sent his son to be brought up in Becket's household. It was often said that Becket and the king were 'but one heart and one mind'.

Henry II wanted to gain control over the English Church, which often ignored him in favour of the Pope. In particular, churchmen guilty of crimes could claim 'benefit of clergy', allowing them to avoid trial in the King's courts. Henry II wanted this to change. In 1162 Henry persuaded his loyal friend Thomas Becket to become Archbishop of Canterbury and carry out his reforms to the Church. However, once Becket became Archbishop, he became intensely religious. He stopped drinking and took to wearing an uncomfortable shirt made of animal hair to show his godliness. Instead of standing up for Henry II, Becket refused to take orders from him. Instead of defending the crown, Becket defended the Church. Henry was furious at this betrayal.

When the king wanted his son Henry crowned King of England early to ensure a peaceful succession, Becket refused. And when the king tried to force Becket to obey him, Becket went behind his back and won the support of the Pope. Matters became serious when Becket lost his temper in the King's court and called Henry's illegitimate brother a 'bastard'. Becket had to go into exile in France for four years.

On his return to England in 1170, Becket tried to **excommunicate** bishops who had been loyal to the king. This was the last straw for Henry, and tradition says he shouted "will nobody rid me of this turbulent priest?" Whatever he actually said, four knights overheard the king, and interpreted his outburst as an order.

The four knights travelled to Canterbury Cathedral, where they found Thomas Becket preparing for an evening service. They asked Becket to leave the church, but he refused. A struggle broke out: one knight swung his sword at Becket and chopped off part of his skull. The Archbishop fell to the ground and, according to a witness, his brains spilled out over the cathedral floor.

The people of England were appalled. Thomas Becket quickly became a Christian **martyr**, Canterbury became a site of pilgrimage, and in 1173 the Pope made Becket a saint. Henry II realised he had made a great mistake in causing the death of his once great friend, and needed to seek forgiveness. In 1174, he walked to Canterbury in bare feet and a hair shirt, and once there, the king was whipped by the monks and bishops of Canterbury before spending the night sleeping beside Becket's shrine. It must have been a very unusual sight for the king's subjects.

Henry's last days

Henry II's reign, which had started so well, ended in sadness. Three of Henry II's eldest sons were angry that he would not share control of the Angevin Empire and, along with their mother Queen Eleanor, they led an uprising against his rule. The revolt failed, and Henry II threw Eleanor in prison. Henry never properly made peace with his sons and they continued to rebel against his rule. Deserted by his family, Henry died in 1189, supposedly of a broken heart.

Illustration of the murder of Thomas Becket from an illuminated manuscript

Canterbury Cathedral, England

Check your understanding

1. Why was it said that Henry II and Thomas Becket were 'but one heart and one mind'?
2. How did Becket change when he became Archbishop of Canterbury?
3. What was the final straw that caused Becket to go into exile in France for four years?
4. How did Henry II cause four knights to travel to Canterbury and kill Thomas Becket?
5. What did Henry II do in response to Thomas Becket's death?

King John (1199–1216)

When Henry II died in 1189, he had two surviving sons. Richard, the elder, was crowned king. He was hugely popular, and was known as 'Richard the Lionheart' for his bravery on the battlefield.

As soon as Richard was crowned king, he went on a crusade to the Holy Land. With his brother away, John tried to steal Richard's crown and become King of England. While returning from his crusade through central Europe, Richard was imprisoned by Duke Leopold of Austria. John was asked to pay his brother's ransom but refused. He even told the English people that Richard had been killed on his crusade. In 1194, Richard returned to England, and in a show of mercy he forgave his brother John for betraying him.

John as king

Five years later, Richard I died while fighting in France, so John became king. King John's nephew, Arthur, also had a claim to the throne, so John captured Arthur and imprisoned him in a castle in France. The young prince was never seen again: some claimed John tied Arthur to a stone and drowned him in the River Seine.

Like his father, John had fierce arguments with the Church. He was extremely stubborn, and disagreed with the Pope about who should be the next Archbishop of Canterbury. In 1209 the Pope excommunicated John and ordered an '**interdict**', meaning that no English church could hold services, marry couples, baptise children or bury dead bodies. For five years, English churches were locked to worshippers, and the people were furious: because they were unable to go to church, they feared they would go straight to hell.

19th-century depiction of King John

Military losses

The King of France was keen to get his hands on John's territories in France. While his brother Richard had won startling victories defending this land, King John nearly lost it all.

In a series of defeats, John lost Brittany, Anjou and – most embarrassingly – his family's ancestral homeland of Normandy. By 1204, he had lost one-third of his entire kingdom, and had earned the nickname John 'Softsword' and 'Lackland' for his unsuccessful record on the battlefield. In 1214, John assembled a large army to win back his land in France, but experienced a crushing defeat at the Battle of Bouvines.

The English barons were not happy. They had paid enormous taxes for John to raise his army, but he kept on losing. In addition, King John ruled England as a cruel **tyrant**. In 1203, King John took 22 knights who had supported Arthur's claim to the throne, locked them in a dungeon in

The ruins of Corfe Castle in Dorset, England

Corfe Castle, and left them to starve. When John fell out with his court favourite, William de Braose, he invaded William's lands, drove him into exile in Ireland, and starved his wife and son to death.

Magna Carta and civil war

In 1215, the barons marched to London to meet King John and demand that he change his ways. They met him at a meadow beside the River Thames called Runnymede, and confronted him with a list of demands. These included not raising tax without the barons' permission; not imprisoning people without a fair trial (a principle known as **Habeas Corpus**); and not trying to control the English Church. John signed the paper by royal seal, and it became known as '**Magna Carta**', Latin for the 'Great Charter'.

True to his character, no sooner had John signed Magna Carta then he claimed it was invalid. The barons were furious, marched to London, and declared that John should no longer rule as king. By the autumn of 1215, England was engulfed in civil war, and King John spent a year laying siege to the castles of rebellious barons around England.

In October 1216, John was campaigning in East Anglia, and one evening feasted on peaches and cider. He went to bed suffering an upset stomach, and died during the night. The civil war was over, and few mourned the death of this stubborn and selfish king. The monks particularly disliked him, caricaturing him in their books as lazy and luxury loving, gloating over his gold and jewels, and staying in bed until midday.

> **Fact**
>
> After King John's death, one monk wrote: "Hell is a foul place, but will be made fouler by the presence of King John."

However, King John's reign did leave a lasting legacy in the form of Magna Carta. Future monarchs were expected to vow that they would never rule as a tyrant by reconfirming the agreement made between King John and his barons. Magna Carta has become a foundational document for English political rights and freedoms.

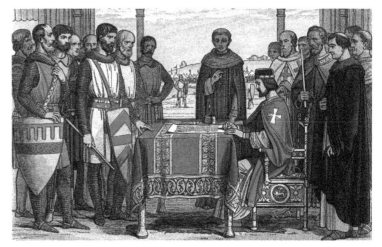

Modern illustration of King John signing Magna Carta

Check your understanding

1. What is King John believed to have done to his nephew Arthur, and why?

2. Why were the people of England so angry about the interdict of 1209?

3. How did King John treat those he disliked or who betrayed him?

4. What are some of the promises included in Magna Carta?

5. How did Magna Carta have a lasting legacy following the death of King John?

Edward I (1272–1307)

Edward I's father, Henry III, spent much of his reign fighting with his barons. For this reason Edward was raised on the battlefield. At the age of 24, he won a great victory for his father at the Battle of Evesham.

Edward was set for more adventures, and embarked on a crusade to the Holy Land. While in the city of Acre in 1272, an assassin tried to kill him in his bedroom. Edward killed the assassin, but was stabbed with a poisoned dagger and very nearly died. Later that year he received news that his father Henry III was dead. Edward's adventure was over, and the crusader prince returned home to become King of England.

Standing 6 feet 2 inches, King Edward was known by his troops as 'Longshanks', meaning 'long legs'. After the unhappy reigns of his father Henry III and his grandfather King John, the charismatic Edward I was welcomed by the English people. He had good looks, a booming voice, and a loving marriage to his Spanish Queen Eleanor of Castile, who bore him 16 children.

Conquest of Wales

However, Edward I could also be horribly cruel. His father had lost land to Wales and Scotland, and they were becoming troublesome neighbours. During his coronation, Edward I removed his crown and claimed that he would not wear it again until he had recovered the lands his father lost.

Since the Norman invasion, Wales had been ruled by princes, who were expected to pay homage to the King of England. However, a Welsh prince named Llywelyn ap Gruffyd had taken control of the whole of the country, and named himself **Prince of Wales**. Prince Llywelyn did not attend Edward's coronation in 1272, and refused to pay homage to the new king. For Edward I, this meant war.

King Edward invaded Wales and defeated Llywelyn in 1277, stripping him of his power but sparing his life. War broke out again in 1282. This time Llywelyn was killed in battle, his head was carried to London on a lanceman's pike, and kept on a spike at the Tower of London for 15 years.

Llywelyn's brother Dafydd carried on fighting, but was captured by Edward's forces a few months later. He was sentenced for high **treason**, and a horrible new death was used for his execution. Dafydd was dragged through the streets by a horse, hanged until almost dead, disembowelled with his entrails burned in front of him, and then cut into four pieces which were sent around England. This gruesome execution became known as being '**hanged, drawn and quartered**'.

By 1283, Edward had conquered Wales, and set about building a series of enormous castles across the country. He also made his eldest son and heir 'Prince of Wales', a practice that continues to this day.

19th-century depiction of King Edward I

Fact

Five of Edward and Eleanor's daughter's survived into adulthood: Eleanor, Joan, Margaret, Mary and Elizabeth. The princesses were given a remarkable education, including reading, recitation, embroidery, music, hunting, riding, falconry and chess.

Harlech Castle, built by Edward I after his conquest of Wales

Conquest of Scotland

Edward then turned his attention towards Scotland, where the king, John Balliol, was also refusing to pay him homage. In 1296, Edward declared himself King of both England and Scotland, and took his army north to invade.

The brutality of Edward's army towards the Scots is infamous. Edward I took just 21 days to conquer the country, slaughtering the Scottish rebels and earning his nickname the 'Hammer of the Scots'. King John Balliol was stripped of his crown. Edward took the ancient **Stone of Destiny**, on which Scottish kings had been crowned for 400 years, from Scotland and placed it underneath his throne in Westminster Abbey.

However, Edward was quickly running out of money, and did not have the funds to keep control of his newly conquered Scotland. Rebellions broke out, led by a charismatic Scottish leader called William Wallace. Wallace was captured in 1305 and hanged, drawn and quartered. The following year, a nobleman called Robert the Bruce was crowned King of Scotland, so Edward led yet another army north to defeat the Scots. He died during the march. Scotland remained independent from England for another 400 years.

William Wallace statue in Aberdeen, Scotland

The model Parliament

To raise money for his campaigns in Scotland and Wales, Edward called for **Parliament** to meet in Westminster in 1295. Two elected representatives from each county were to attend, along with all England's bishops and noblemen. As Edward's request stated, "What touches all should be approved of all." This was the first time a king had sought the agreement of his people before taxing them, and Edward I's Parliament became the model for all future kings.

Fact

Robert the Bruce decided to fight back against Edward I after his own sister, Mary Bruce, was hung outside her castle walls in a wooden cage by English soldiers.

Today's Houses of Parliament in London, England

Check your understanding

1. Why did Edward I decide to invade Wales?
2. What did Edward I do to punish Dafydd ap Gruffyd?
3. How did Edward I earn the nickname the 'Hammer of the Scots'?
4. Why did Edward I fail to bring Scotland under English control?
5. Why did Edward I call for Parliament to meet in 1295?

Henry V (1413–22)

Henry V's father Henry IV was an unpopular king, who spent much of his reign putting down rebellions. He died from a terrible skin condition, which was possibly leprosy.

Henry V was crowned king in 1413, and worked hard to win the support of the English people. He restored titles, castles and lands to nobles who had opposed his father. To meet his subjects and make sure his laws were being kept, Henry V travelled the country in a grand procession. Unusually for a medieval king, Henry V learned to read and write in English, which greatly aided royal administration. He was also the first King of England to conduct his court in English, not French.

War in France

During Henry V's reign, the '**Hundred Years War**' was being fought between England and France. England lost almost all of its land in France, and its only remaining territory was the port town of **Calais**.

Portrait of King Henry V

However, during this period, France was ruled by a mentally unstable king called Charles VI, and was engulfed in civil war. Henry V spied this as a perfect opportunity to gain back land in France. He presented his plan to Parliament, and its members gave their full support to an invasion, doubling taxes to pay for it. In August 1415, Henry V crossed the English Channel with 12 000 men, and successfully took the French port of Harfleur after a one-month siege.

> ### Fact
> King Charles VI of France believed he was made out of glass, and feared that he might smash at any point.

Agincourt: the impossible victory

After his victory at Harfleur, things turned against Henry V. Some of his army had been killed during the siege of Harfleur, and many were sent home suffering from a disease called **dysentery**. With what was left of his army, Henry decided to march from Harfleur to Calais, where they could spend the winter.

They were met with appalling weather, and for almost a month Henry's 8000 men trudged through constant rain with very few supplies. They were cold, weak, wounded and hungry. Then came some terrible news: an army of 12 000 heavily armed French soldiers was waiting for them on the road to Calais.

The two armies met on a narrow strip of high ground between two forests. The English soldiers arrived first, and they established their defensive line the night before the battle by digging two-metre sharpened wooden stakes – called **palings** – into the ground. Henry positioned his **men-at-arms** behind the palings, and the English and Welsh longbowmen hid in the forests on either side. And there, Henry's weak and outnumbered army waited for the French attack.

The battle began on the morning of 25 October, St Crispin's Day. The enormous French army advanced with 9000 men-at-arms. However, they did not realise how wet the ground was and, funnelled by the forests on either side, many got stuck in the mud. At this point, the English archers rained a storm of arrows down on the sitting target of French soldiers. Once they had run out of arrows, the English soldiers charged out of the forest and from behind their palings, attacking the French with axes and swords. Henry V led the charge and was knocked off his horse, but continued to fight.

The French were massacred: around 5000 are thought to have died, compared with 1600 Englishmen. The Battle of Agincourt is still remembered today as one of the greatest victories in English military history.

Victory in France

Henry V won a series of victories in France following the Battle of Agincourt. By 1420, Henry V was closing in on the capital city Paris. At this point he could have won the French throne by force, but instead Henry V signed the Treaty of Troyes with King Charles.

The treaty agreed that Henry V would marry Charles' daughter Catharine and, on Charles' death, Henry V would become King of France. However, in 1422 Henry V died of dysentery while on campaign. Had he lived just one month more, Henry V would have outlived Charles VI and become King of both England and France.

Modern illustration of English archers at the Battle of Agincourt

Longbowmen

Two metres in length, **longbows** could fire with great range and frequency. They played a pivotal role in England's victories over the French during the Hundred Years War. One king, Edward III, made it compulsory for all Englishmen between the ages of 15 and 60 to practise archery on Sundays and holy days. He even banned sports such as football and hockey, which might distract men from their archery practice.

The war with France took an unexpected turn in 1425 when a 13-year-old French peasant girl named **Joan of Arc** had a religious vision telling her to drive out the English. Dressed as a knight, she amassed a following and led a series of victories, including at the Battle of Patay, which was as significant a victory for the French as Agincourt was for the English. However, in 1431, age 19, she was put on trial for heresy, witchcraft and cross-dressing, and was burned at the stake.

Modern reenactment of a medieval longbowman

Check your understanding
1. What did Henry V learn to do, which was unusual for an English king during this period?
2. What gave Henry V the perfect opportunity to invade France in 1415?
3. In what condition was Henry V's English army before the Battle of Agincourt?
4. Why were English longbowmen crucial to the English victory at Agincourt?
5. Why was Henry V never able to claim his title as King of both England and France?

Medieval queens

During the medieval period, it was rare for women to hold political power. Noble women were first and foremost supposed to give birth to healthy male children.

However, some medieval queens were exceptions to this general rule. These remarkable individuals rose above the expectations set by their gender and wielded considerable power over medieval England.

Eleanor of Aquitaine

Eleanor of Aquitaine was the eldest child of the Duke of Aquitaine – an enormous territory stretching across the south-west of France. When her father died, Eleanor inherited his lands.

Attractive, well-educated and enormously wealthy, the 15-year-old Eleanor became the most sought after bride in medieval Europe. Before long, she was married to King Louis VII of France. Louis VII, who was slow-witted and lacked charm, was not a good match for the high-spirited and intelligent Eleanor.

In 1147, Louis VII joined the Second Crusade, and Eleanor insisted on accompanying her husband to the Holy Land. However, once they arrived in the Holy Land, Eleanor questioned Louis' decision-making and refused to accompany him south towards Jerusalem. Louis was enraged by his wife's disobedience, and they divorced in 1152.

Eight weeks after her divorce, Eleanor shocked medieval Europe by marrying the heir to the English throne, Henry, Duke of Normandy. When her new husband was crowned Henry II in 1154 (see Chapter 1, this unit), Eleanor became Queen of England. This marriage was more successful, and together they had five sons.

As the years went on, Eleanor and her strong-willed husband Henry II began to quarrel. In 1168 Eleanor left England for France, to rule her ancestral homeland of Aquitaine on Henry II's behalf. There she developed a glamorous court, which was celebrated in poems and songs across Europe for its displays of chivalry. However, in 1174 Eleanor was arrested for helping to plot a revolt against Henry II's rule, and imprisoned for 15 years.

But Queen Eleanor's political career was not over. When Henry II died in 1189, Eleanor's favourite son, Richard I, became king. One of his first acts was to order the release of his

> **Fact**
>
> Medieval writers frequently debated whether the virtues of men and women differed. In 1405, Christine de Pizan, one of Europe's first female professional writers, wrote *The Book of the City of Ladies*. By using examples of well-known women such as the Queen of Sheba and Helen of Troy, Pizan argued that all women should be given a more significant place in society. She encouraged readers to remember that women could be capable of greatness.

Effigy of Eleanor of Aquitaine in Fontevraud Abbey, France

67-year-old mother from prison. When Richard left England to fight in the Third Crusade, Queen Eleanor ruled England on his behalf as his **regent**.

Richard I died in 1199, and Eleanor transferred her loyalty to her youngest son King John (see Chapter 2, this unit). Queen Eleanor spent the last years of her life travelling through France and Spain negotiating alliances on his behalf. When Eleanor died in 1204 at the age of 82, she was one of the most powerful figures, male or female, in all of Europe.

Isabella of France

Isabella of France was just 12 years old when she married Edward II (son of Edward I, see Chapter 3, this unit) in 1308. Unfortunately for Isabella, her new husband was already in love with a male courtier named Piers Gaveston. Edward II and Gaveston adored each other, although nobody today knows for sure whether their relationship was physical.

In 1312, a group of barons captured Piers Gaveston and had him executed. After Gaveston's death, Edward II and Isabella's relationship improved, and they had four children. Edward came to admire his wife's intelligence and judgment, and relied on her advice. However, before long Edward II gained a new favourite called Hugh Despenser. Despenser was a greedy and sinister nobleman, much hated by the rest of England's barons. Queen Isabella despised him.

In 1325, Edward II sent his wife Isabella to her homeland of France to negotiate a treaty on his behalf. Once in France, Isabella fell in love with an English knight named Roger Mortimer. Together, they began to organise a rebellion against Edward II. Isabella and Mortimer raised an army and invaded England in September 1326. They captured Hugh Despenser, and had him hanged, drawn and quartered. Edward II was arrested and imprisoned in Berkeley Castle – making Isabella the only queen in English history to **depose** her own husband. If the rumours that later emerged are to be believed, Edward II died a horrific death.

Isabella made her 14-year-old son Edward III king, but ruled on his behalf alongside her lover Mortimer. Once Edward III grew older, however, he had Mortimer executed and his mother imprisoned. However, Isabella slowly won back her son's favour, and lived in freedom for almost 30 more years, dying at the age of 63. Isabella's ability to wield political power earned her both hatred and respect in England, where she was nicknamed 'She Wolf of France'.

> ## Fact
>
> At Edward II's coronation feast, the king chose not to sit beside his new Queen Isabella, but instead sat next to his favourite courtier Piers Gaveston. Isabella was humiliated by her husband's behaviour, and her family were outraged.

15th-century illustration, showing Queen Isabella leading her army at Hereford

---

Check your understanding

1. Why were women unlikely to hold political power during the medieval period?
2. In what ways was Eleanor's marriage to Henry II more successful than her marriage to Louis VII?
3. How did Eleanor wield power during the reigns of her sons, Richard I and King John?
4. Which two male courtiers became Edward II's favourites, and what happened to each of them?
5. What did Isabella of France do which makes her unique among English queens?

Unit 4: Medieval kingship
Knowledge organiser

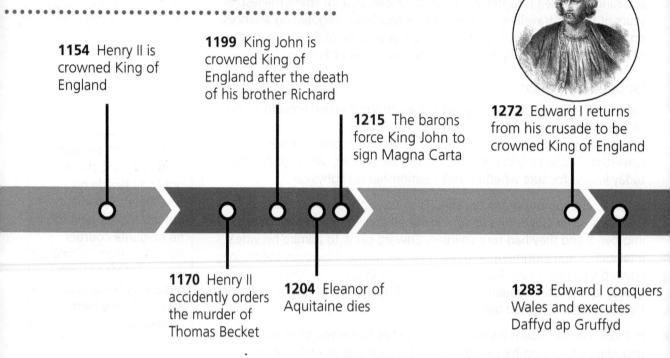

1154 Henry II is crowned King of England

1199 King John is crowned King of England after the death of his brother Richard

1215 The barons force King John to sign Magna Carta

1272 Edward I returns from his crusade to be crowned King of England

1170 Henry II accidently orders the murder of Thomas Becket

1204 Eleanor of Aquitaine dies

1283 Edward I conquers Wales and executes Daffyd ap Gruffyd

Key vocabulary

Angevin Empire An Empire ruled by Henry II, stretching from Scotland to the Pyrenees

Aquitaine Large medieval Duchy covering south-west France, ruled by Queen Eleanor

Calais French port town, which for two centuries was an English territory

Depose To suddenly or forcefully remove a monarch from power

Dysentery An infection of the intestines that causes severe diarrhoea

Excommunication Expulsion from the Catholic Church by the Pope

Habeas Corpus The principle that no person should be imprisoned without first having a fair trial

Hanged, drawn and quartered A gruesome execution, often used against those who commit treason

Hundred Years War A long conflict between England and France beginning in the 14th century

Interdict A law ruled by the Pope which temporarily shuts down the Church in a country or area

Longbow A two-metre bow, used to great effect by the English during the late medieval period

Magna Carta A series of promises that King John made to limit his power; meaning 'Great Charter'

Men-at-arms Heavily armed medieval soldiers on horseback, but not necessarily feudal knights

Martyr A person who is killed for their beliefs, often religious

Palings A barrier made from pointed wooden or metal poles to defend against cavalry charges

Parliament A collection of people representing all of England, who approve or refuse laws

Prince of Wales A title granted since the reign of Edward I to the heir to the English throne

Enquiry Question: What qualities were required to be an effective medieval monarch?

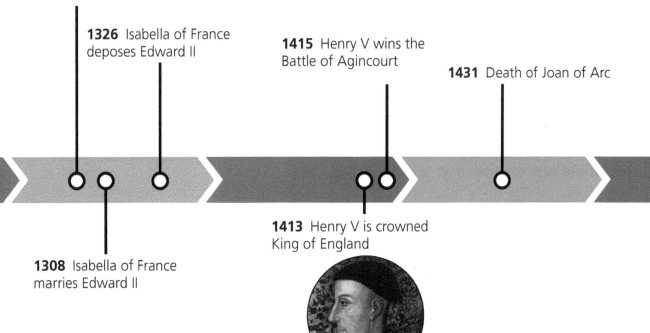

1305 Edward I executes the rebel Scottish leader William Wallace

1326 Isabella of France deposes Edward II

1415 Henry V wins the Battle of Agincourt

1431 Death of Joan of Arc

1308 Isabella of France marries Edward II

1413 Henry V is crowned King of England

Key people

Edward I English king known as the 'Hammer of the Scots'

Eleanor of Aquitaine Wife of Henry II and one of the most powerful women in medieval Europe

Henry II English king who accidently ordered the murder of his own Archbishop of Canterbury

Henry V English king who won the Battle of Agincourt

Isabella of France English queen who deposed her own husband, Edward II

Joan of Arc French peasant girl who led armies into battle against the English

King John English king seen as a tyrant who was forced to sign Magna Carta

Llywelyn ap Gruffyd The last Prince of Wales, prior to its conquest by Edward I

Thomas Becket A medieval Archbishop of Canterbury who was killed for his opposition to King Henry II

William Wallace A rebel knight who led the resistance to Edward I's conquest of Scotland

Key vocabulary

Regent Someone who is appointed to rule on behalf of a monarch, when the monarch is too young, infirm or absent to rule

Stone of Destiny A large block of sandstone historically used for the coronation of Scottish monarchs

Treason A crime against your own people, nation or monarch

Tyrant A ruler who refuses to share their power, and governs in a cruel and oppressive way

The Black Death

During the 1340s, stories started to arrive in Europe of a dreadful disease ravaging the populations of far off lands in India and China. Such stories were common, but this one happened to be true.

The **Black Death** first hit European trading towns, such as Venice, in 1347. The first recorded deaths in England occurred in June 1348 at the port town of Melcombe Regis in Dorset. Within two years, this horrifying disease had killed between one-third and half of England's population.

The pestilence

We now call this plague the 'Black Death', but people in medieval England would have called it the '**pestilence**' or the 'Great Mortality'. The first symptoms were large swellings known as '**buboes**', which appeared in victims' armpits and between their legs, and were said to resemble an onion.

The buboes then spread across the body, followed by blue or black blotches. Sufferers then started to vomit and spit blood, suffer from seizures, and their breath turned foul and stinking. After two to three days of horrific suffering, they would be dead. Occasionally, the buboes would burst, emitting a rancid smelling pus. However, this was a good sign, as it often meant the body was fighting back against the disease and might overpower it. Named after the buboes, which were its first symptom, this variant of the disease is now known as the '**bubonic plague**'.

There was also a more lethal variant called the '**pneumonic plague**', which was spread through the breath. This version of the plague attacked the lungs, giving sufferers a fever, and leading them to choke to death with a bloody froth bubbling at the mouth.

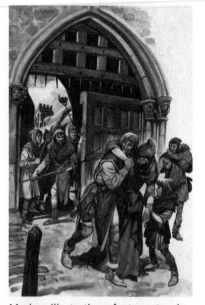

Modern illustration of a town turning away visitors during the Black Death

Explanations for the plague

Today, we know that the bubonic plague was caused by bacteria, and was spread by fleas living on black rats. The rats would have lived on merchant ships, and run to shore across rigging ropes that attached a ship to the harbour. However, during the medieval period, people had no understanding of what was causing great swathes of their population to die.

The explanations that people did devise show the power of religion and **superstition** in the medieval mind. Most people believed the plague was punishment sent down by God, who had been angered by greed and sin on Earth. Others believed that it was caused by an alignment of stars and planets. In Europe, some claimed that the **Jews** who lived among the Christian population were poisoning their wells, leading to mass killings

A black rat running along a rigging rope to a ship.

of Jewish communities in Germany and France. Some even thought that poisonous air, known as '**miasma**', was spreading the disease.

Treatments

With no understanding of what was causing the disease, ideas for treatments were equally far-fetched. Remedies included drinking vinegar, avoiding moist food, bleeding, and taking medicine made out of anything from crushed jewels to insects. Some believed that they could sweat out the disease, so sat between two raging fires, or wrapped themselves in furs to induce sweating.

Medicine in medieval Europe was very basic. Doctors would place a frog on the buboes in an attempt to absorb the poison, or even a severed pigeon head. Some doctors came to realise that bursting the buboes could cause the illness to stop, and became increasingly skilled at doing this with a small lance to allow the pus to seep out.

However, sufferers kept on dying. The countryside was littered with corpses in the fields and on the roadside. Whole communities became ghost towns almost overnight. The plague was particularly bad in large towns and cities, where corpses were thrown into mass graves, often little more than ditches with a thin layer of earth to cover the dead.

The Scots realised the English people were in distress, and invaded England in 1350. However, the Scottish soldiers soon caught the plague themselves, and when they retreated north of the border, they spread the plague to Scotland. Not even the clergy or royal family were safe from the plague. Three Archbishops of Canterbury died in quick succession, and King Edward III's daughter died while travelling to meet her new husband in Spain.

Fact

A recently excavated mass grave near the Tower of London revealed plague sufferers buried five deep.

Flagellants

During the Black Death, a religious sect called '**flagellants**' took to travelling England in procession, whipping themselves in punishment for their sins. Their reasoning was that if they punished themselves, God would not see the need to punish them also with the plague. However, by exposing their wounds and travelling the country, flagellants probably contributed to the spread of the plague. They were condemned by Pope Clement VI in 1349.

Illustration showing a procession of flagellants

Check your understanding

1. What proportion of England's population was killed by the Black Death?
2. What were the symptoms of the bubonic plague?
3. What was the most common explanation for the Black Death?
4. How were dead bodies dealt with in towns and cities during the Black Death?
5. Why did flagellants think that whipping themselves would save them from the Black Death?

The Peasants' Revolt

By 1351, the worst of the Black Death was over in England. In some historians' estimates, it had killed around two million people.

Having lost such a large proportion of the country's population, landowners found it increasingly difficult to find enough peasants to work their land. Peasants knew that their services were in high demand, and started moving from farm to farm asking for higher wages. Edward III tried to stop this in 1351 with the **Statute of Labourers**, which fixed peasant wages at the pre-Black Death levels. However, peasants and landowners alike paid little attention to the law.

Class conflict

Enterprising peasants with money to spare were able to buy up the land and empty houses belonging to plague victims for rock bottom prices. This new class of landowners became known as **yeomen**, meaning a peasant with up to 100 acres of farmland. Yeoman farmers threatened the feudal hierarchy and the status of its traditional landlords. Some survivors of the plague also turned against the authority of the Catholic Church, which had been powerless to explain or prevent the Black Death.

Power was slowly moving to the people, and the nobles were not happy. In 1363, the **Sumptuary Laws** were passed, laying out in detail what different classes were allowed to wear. Gold cloth and purple silk were reserved for the royal family; lords could wear fur and precious stones; and knights could wear fur-trimmed cloaks. Peasants were banned from wearing anything except plain cloth costing less than 12 pence a length.

Wat Tyler's rebellion

Tensions between the lords and the people came to a head in 1381. At this time the 14-year-old King Richard II ruled England. However, he left much of the government of England to his uncle John of Gaunt, an unpopular nobleman with little concern for the common people.

To help pay for the Hundred Years War against France, John of Gaunt established the **Poll Tax**. This was a one-off tax of 4p to be paid by all adults over the age of 14 (poll means head, so it was literally a tax 'per head' on the English people). As the same price was to be paid by all people, rich or poor, the Poll Tax was deeply unpopular among England's peasants.

15th-century manuscript depicting the meeting of Wat Tyler and John Ball in 1381

On 30 May 1381, a royal official arrived in the Essex town of Brentwood to collect the new tax. The Essex peasants refused to pay, killing the official's clerks and sending him fleeing back to London. Within three days the whole county of Essex was in open rebellion against the king, and thousands of Essex peasants decided to march on London.

At the same time, a yeoman named Wat Tyler organised around 4000 peasants to march on London from the nearby county of Kent. Armed with bows, clubs and axes, the rebels reached London on 13 June. Here a radical preacher, John Ball, rallied them with a speech, in which he asked: "When Adam delved and Eve span, who was then the gentleman?"

Once inside London, the rebels stormed Newgate and Westminster prisons, and burned John of Gaunt's sumptuous **Savoy Palace** to the ground. One of the most unpopular figures in the king's government was the Archbishop of Canterbury, Simon Sudbury. The peasants executed him on Tower Hill alongside the Lord High Treasurer, Sir Robert Hales, and their heads were placed on spikes and paraded around London.

Great Coxwell Barn, Oxfordshire. Medieval peasants were expected to pay tax to the Church and their landlord in 'tithe barns' such as this

Richard's response

To bring an end to this chaos, Richard II agreed to meet the rebels outside London at a place called Smithfield on Saturday 15 June 1381. Their leader, Wat Tyler, rode out to negotiate with Richard. Accounts vary as to what happened next. Some say Tyler attacked Richard's men, others that he rudely spat on the ground. Either way, a struggle ensued during which Tyler was run through with a sword and killed.

Richard seized the initiative, and promised to agree to the peasants' demands so long as they returned to their towns and villages. They duly did so, but the king had little intention of keeping his promise. Richard II went back on every concession he had made to the rebels, and 200 of their leaders were tracked down and hanged. The **Peasants' Revolt** may have been a failure, but feudal England had been challenged. Over the next two centuries, England's peasants gradually became freemen, and were no longer tied to working for their feudal lords.

Fact

Contemporary court documents record that Johanna Ferrour was the "chief perpetrator and leader of the rebellious evil-doers from Kent". She personally ordered the beheading of Simon Sudbury and Robert Hales, and took part in the burning of Savoy Palace while distributing chests of gold among the rebels.

Check your understanding

1. How did the government respond to the growing wealth and power of medieval peasants?
2. Why was the Poll Tax so unpopular among medieval peasants?
3. What parts of England did the peasants who took place in the revolt come from?
4. What did the peasants do once they reached London?
5. How did Wat Tyler die?

The Wars of the Roses

Crowned in 1423, Henry VI was England's youngest ever king at just nine months old. For the first 16 years of his life, a royal council governed England on his behalf.

Illustration depicting the Lancastrian King Henry VI

When Henry VI came of age, he fell well short of the great expectations set by his father Henry V, the hero of Agincourt.

England had been steadily losing its French territories to a newly powerful French king, Charles VII. When England lost Normandy, the 18-year-old Henry VI was expected to fulfil his duty and lead the English army into war. Instead, he sent his cousin to do the job. Henry VI hated the idea of war, and was the first medieval king never to lead his army on the battlefield. He preferred books and churches to swords and armour. Many of Henry VI's noblemen believed their king was, quite simply, a coward.

By 1450, England's French empire was once again reduced to the small port town of Calais. That year, a rebellion broke out in London, with three days of open fighting in the streets led by a rebel named Jack Cade. The rebels dragged a former minister of the king from the Tower of London and beheaded him.

To make matters worse, in 1453 King Henry VI suffered the first of many bouts of mental illness. For a year he was completely unresponsive to anything around him, and had to be cared for like a newborn child.

The Yorkist threat

Henry VI was clearly incapable of ruling, so power passed to a group of powerful noblemen. Chief among them was the king's cousin, a wealthy nobleman called Richard, Duke of York. However, Henry VI's French wife, Margaret of Anjou, despised the overly powerful Duke of York. Queen Margaret was a formidable leader, and she began to organise opposition to the Duke of York.

Symbol of the white York rose

This led to two rival factions forming in the king's court. The followers of the Duke of York, known as the 'House of York', were on one side; the supporters of the king led by Queen Margaret, known as the 'House of Lancaster', were on the other. Although they did not use them at the time, the two sides are today identified by two roses – a white rose for the **Yorkists**, and a red rose for the **Lancastrians**.

Symbol of the red Lancaster rose

Outbreak of war

In 1459, Margaret of Anjou declared Richard, Duke of York a traitor, and war broke out between the House of York and the House of Lancaster.

The **Wars of the Roses** had begun. Queen Margaret was unafraid to fight defending what she believed was hers, and took control of the Lancastrian forces, declaring "I will either conquer or be conquered with you." She defeated the Duke of York at the battle of Wakefield in December 1460. The Duke was cornered on the battlefield by Lancastrian troops, and beheaded. Margaret ordered that his head should be placed on a spike outside the gates of the city of York and adorned with a paper crown.

However, Queen Margaret's success did not last. The people of London refused to allow her into their city, and Margaret had to withdraw to the north of England. Meanwhile, with Richard, Duke of York now dead, his son Edward took on the leadership of the House of York. Aged only 18, he was everything that King Henry VI was not: standing 6 feet 4 inches tall, Edward of York was a proven warrior on the battlefield and a charismatic leader.

In March 1461, Edward of York was crowned King Edward IV of England. To confirm his rule, the new king marched north to finish off the Lancastrians, and won a victory at the brutal Battle of Towton on 29 March. Henry VI and Queen Margaret fled into exile in Scotland, and Edward IV secured his place as the first Yorkist King of England.

> **Fact**
>
> Henry VI was present at the Second Battle of St Albans in 1461, but the king spent the battle singing to himself while sitting under a tree.

Battle of Towton

Today it is largely forgotten, but the Battle of Towton is probably the single bloodiest battle ever fought on British soil. The Yorkist and the Lancastrian forces each numbered around 50 000 men, and they faced each other on a freezing cold morning in March.

Already brutalised by two years of fighting, ideas of chivalry had disappeared in England. An extreme level of bloodlust marked the battle. Skulls found at the site were covered with more than 20 wounds, suggesting that soldiers mutilated the dead bodies of their enemies. By the end of the day, 8000 Lancastrians lay dead, alongside 5000 Yorkists, and the snow-covered field was stained red with blood.

Modern illustration of the Battle of Towton

Check your understanding

1. In what way was Henry VI different from his father, Henry V?
2. Why did many nobles, such as the Duke of York, believe Henry VI was incapable of ruling England?
3. Who led the House of Lancaster at the beginning of the Wars of the Roses?
4. Who was crowned as the first Yorkist King of England in March 1461?
5. What can be learned about the Battle of Towton from the skeletons that have been found on the site?

Yorkist rule

Aside from a short exile in France, Edward IV ruled England from 1461 to 1483. Overshadowed by the chaos of the wars that surrounded him, Edward IV is sometimes called England's 'forgotten king'.

As king, Edward was popular and charming, and brought a brief spell of prosperity to England. His power depended upon the support of his allies, and chief among them was the Earl of Warwick. Warwick had groomed Edward to be king from an early age and was the true power behind the throne. One French visitor recalled at the time, "England has two kings, Warwick, and another whose name I have forgotten."

The Kingmaker

Edward IV wanted to break free from the control of Warwick. A romantic at heart, in 1464 he secretly married his true love, a commoner named Elizabeth Woodville. Such a marriage was unheard of for a king, who was expected to form a tactical alliance by marrying into another royal family. When the Earl of Warwick found out about Edward's marriage, he was furious.

In 1469, Warwick switched sides to the House of Lancaster. A year later he invaded England with Margaret of Anjou, who had been living in exile in France. Edward IV fled to Flanders, and Warwick made Henry VI king once more, earning his nickname '**The Kingmaker**'. However, Henry VI's second reign lasted for only a year. In 1471 at the Battle of Barnet, Edward IV defeated the Lancastrian army and the Earl of Warwick was killed. Henry VI died in prison, most likely murdered by Edward's soldiers.

For twelve more years, Edward IV ruled England in relative peace. However, in 1483 he caught a cold while fishing, and a few days later died aged just 40 years old.

The princes in the Tower

The death of Edward IV led to one last chapter in the Wars of the Roses. Edward IV had two young sons, aged 12 and 9, who were in Ludlow when their father died. The eldest, named Edward, was due to become King Edward V. His uncle, Richard, the Duke of Gloucester, was chosen to rule as a **protector** on the young king's behalf.

Richard met the princes as they travelled from Ludlow to London, but when they arrived in the capital he imprisoned them in the Tower of London. Richard claimed it was for their own safety, but it soon turned out that the greatest threat to the princes' safety was Richard himself. Richard declared the marriage between his older brother Edward IV and Elizabeth Woodville invalid, ruling out Edward V's claim to the throne. He then had himself crowned King Richard III.

> **Fact**
>
> George, Duke of Clarence was Edward IV's brother. He started the Wars of the Roses fighting for his brother but then betrayed him to fight for Henry VI and Warwick in 1469. George then switched back to Edward's side in 1471. Finally, George was killed for treason in 1478. He was allegedly drowned in a barrel of Malmsey wine.

King Richard III, uncle to the princes in the Tower

The Tower of London where the young princes were imprisoned

Richard III has long been remembered as the greatest villain of this period. In Shakespeare's play *Richard III* (written in 1592), he is depicted as an ugly hunchback with a withered arm, though how far this depiction is true is a source of debate. What is known is that once placed in the Tower, the princes were never seen again. In the years that followed a story emerged that Richard ordered the princes to be suffocated in their beds, smothered with pillows while they slept.

In 1674, labourers working at the Tower of London found a wooden chest hidden beneath a staircase containing two skeletons. They were of two children, one slightly older than the other. The skeletons were pronounced to belong to the two dead princes, and were reinterred at Westminster Abbey. In 1933, the tomb was reopened so that modern forensic methods could finally put the mystery to rest. Professor W. Wright concluded that, on examination of their teeth, the skeletons did belong to two boys, aged around 11 and 13. What is more, he believed a red mark on the facial bones indicated a bloodstain – something commonly caused by suffocation.

Painting of 1831 by French artist Paul Delaroche, titled *The Princes in the Tower*; King Edward V sits to the right.

Back in the summer of 1483, rumours quickly started to spread across England that Richard III had killed the princes. Even in the savage context of the Wars of the Roses, killing your own brother's sons was a step too far. This perhaps explains why so few Englishmen rallied to Richard's cause when, two years later, war with the House of Lancaster resumed.

Check your understanding

1. What role did the Earl of Warwick play when Edward IV became king?
2. Why were Edward VI's subjects, in particular Warwick, so shocked by his marriage?
3. On what basis did Richard III make himself King of England in place of his nephew Edward V?
4. How did Shakespeare depict Richard III in his play, written a century after Richard's death?
5. What did the findings of Professor W. Wright appear to show in 1933?

The Battle of Bosworth Field

By the end of the Wars of the Roses, tracing the rightful claim to the throne in England's tangled royal family was no easy task.

In 1485, an unlikely new claimant to the throne emerged. Brought up in a windswept corner of south-west Wales, Henry Tudor's claim to the throne was tenuous. His Welsh grandfather was a servant to Henry V named Owain ap Maredudd ap Tewdwr. He miraculously married the widowed wife of Henry V in 1432, and anglicised his name to Owen Tudor.

Henry Tudor was a member of the House of Lancaster, and a man of great self-belief. He had spent the previous 14 years of his life exiled in France, preparing his bid for the English throne. Henry was greatly helped by his formidable mother Margaret Beaufort. Margaret was the great-great-granddaughter of Edward III, and married Henry's father at the age of 12. And even that was her second marriage! At the age of 13, Margaret gave birth to Henry Tudor, by which time she was already a widow.

Henry Tudor's mother, Margaret Beaufort

Margaret went on to marry twice more. She was a skilful political operator, moving her support between the Houses of Lancaster and York when it suited her and her beloved son most, waiting for the best moment for Henry to strike.

On 1 August 1485, Henry Tudor landed on the coast of his homeland of Wales, and marched towards England. With a force of just 1000 mostly French soldiers, Henry hoped to gather troops along the way. However, the response of the war-weary nation was not encouraging: as Henry reached the English midlands for his showdown with King Richard III, his forces numbered just 5000 men.

Bosworth Field

Richard III set up camp on 21 August, securing the high ground at a location known as Bosworth Field. His Yorkist army numbered perhaps 10 000 men, and he also had the help of cannon fire, a recent technological advance in medieval warfare.

Outnumbered, and poorly positioned at the foot of the hill in a marshy bog, there was little reason to expect Henry Tudor's Lancastrian forces to win. Richard III led a Yorkist cavalry charge against the Lancastrian forces, but one of Henry's French **pikemen** knocked Richard III off his horse. According to Shakespeare's retelling of the battle, Richard cried out at this moment: "A horse! A horse! My kingdom for a horse!"

Modern illustration of the Battle of Bosworth Field

It was around this time that Lord Stanley, who was Margaret Beaufort's fourth husband, chose to tip the balance of the battle. Stanley had 3000 men, but had so far watched the battle unfold from the sidelines. As the battle started to turn against Richard, Lord Stanley sent in his soldiers to seal the victory for Henry.

All sources agree that Richard III died heroically, fighting off his attackers until he was cornered, overpowered and killed. According to legend, Lord Stanley found Richard III's gold crown in a thorn bush, fished it out and placed it on Henry Tudor's head. Meanwhile, the dead King Richard III was stripped naked and slung on the back of a horse. He was buried in an unmarked grave at Greyfriars Church in Leicester, only to be rediscovered some 500 years later (see box).

Tudor dynasty

After his victory at the Battle of Bosworth Field, Henry Tudor became King Henry VII of England. He ruled in close partnership with his mother Margaret Beaufort. Margaret helped to arrange for Henry VII to marry Elizabeth of York, the daughter of Edward IV and elder sister to the murdered princes in the tower. This well-judged marriage united the Houses of York and Lancaster, finally ending their 30-year feud.

There were rebellions against the new king, but Henry VII saw off his enemies and secured a lasting peace for England. Henry VII's new royal **dynasty**, the **Tudors**, would lead England into a great period of change. For this reason, Henry VII's reign (which ended with his death in 1509) is commonly seen as marking the end of the medieval period in English history.

Fact

To symbolise his union of the two houses, Henry created the **Tudor Rose**: the white rose of York sitting within the red rose of Lancaster.

The king of the car park

To this day, Richard III has his sympathisers. They claim he was a decent and honest king, whose reputation was later smeared by Tudor writers such as William Shakespeare.

Such sympathisers were overjoyed when, in September 2012, archaeologists found what was believed to be Richard III's skeleton beneath a car park in Leicester. Half a century after his death in battle, Richard III was finally given a king's funeral and burial at Leicester Cathedral in March 2015.

Tented site of the dig for Richard III's body under a car park in Leicester

Check your understanding

1. What was Henry Tudor's claim to the throne?
2. Who helped Henry Tudor prepare his bid for the English throne?
3. What happened to Richard III during his cavalry charge against the Lancastrians?
4. What was sensible about Henry VII's decision to marry Elizabeth of York?
5. Who do sympathisers of Richard III believe is responsible for his bad reputation in English history?

Unit 5: Late medieval England
Knowledge organiser

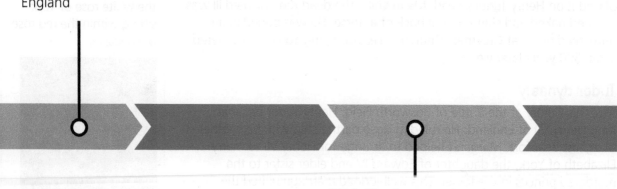

1348 The Black Death hits England

1381 The Peasants' Revolt

Key vocabulary

Black Death A plague that devastated medieval Europe in the 14 century

Buboes Onion-shaped swellings that were usually the first symptom of the Black Death

Bubonic plague The most common variant of the plague, named after the swellings on victims' bodies

Dynasty A succession of powerful people from the same family

Flagellant Member of a religious sect who whipped themselves in punishment for their sins

Jews An ethnic and religious group, belonging to the ancient religion of Judaism

Lancastrian A supporter of King Henry VI, or members of his family, during the Wars of the Roses

Miasma The theory that disease is caused by the spreading smell of a poisonous cloud of 'bad air'

Peasants' Revolt A major uprising across England that took place 30 years after the Black Death

Pestilence Another term for disease, often used to describe the Black Death

Pikemen Soldiers who carried 4-metre-long, steel-headed pikes, used to stop cavalry charges

Pneumonic plague An even more lethal variant of the plague, which attacks the lungs

Poll Tax A flat-rate tax paid by all adults, literally meaning 'per head' of the English people

Protector A nobleman ruling on the behalf of a young monarch until they come of age

Savoy Palace John of Gaunt's sumptuous medieval home, destroyed during the Peasants' Revolt

Statute of Labourers A 1351 law that fixed the maximum wage for peasants at pre-Black Death levels

Sumptuary Laws Rules explaining what clothing different ranks within the feudal system could wear

Superstition The belief in supernatural powers, in place of rational explanation

The Kingmaker A nickname given to the Earl of Warwick during the Wars of the Roses

Tudor Rose A white rose of York sitting within the red rose of Lancaster, symbolising union

Tudors The royal dynasty that ruled England from 1485 to 1603

Wars of the Roses A series of wars between the houses of York and Lancaster, which lasted for 30 years

Yeomen A new class in late medieval England: commoners who farmed their own land

Yorkist A supporter of the Duke of York, and later his sons, during the Wars of the Roses

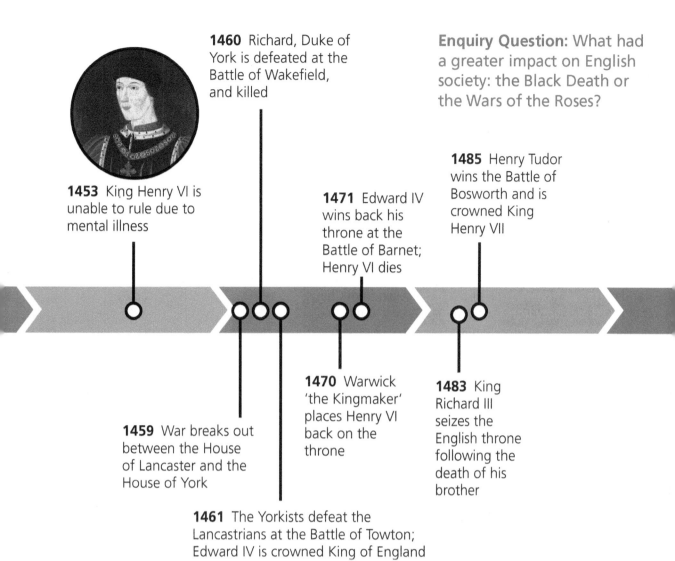

1453 King Henry VI is unable to rule due to mental illness

1460 Richard, Duke of York is defeated at the Battle of Wakefield, and killed

1471 Edward IV wins back his throne at the Battle of Barnet; Henry VI dies

1485 Henry Tudor wins the Battle of Bosworth and is crowned King Henry VII

Enquiry Question: What had a greater impact on English society: the Black Death or the Wars of the Roses?

1459 War breaks out between the House of Lancaster and the House of York

1470 Warwick 'the Kingmaker' places Henry VI back on the throne

1483 King Richard III seizes the English throne following the death of his brother

1461 The Yorkists defeat the Lancastrians at the Battle of Towton; Edward IV is crowned King of England

Key people

Edward IV Son of Richard, Duke of York, he was the first Yorkist King during the Wars of the Roses

Elizabeth of York The elder sister of the murdered princes in the tower, who married Henry Tudor

Elizabeth Woodville The wife of Edward IV, who controversially did not come from a noble family

Henry Tudor The last Lancastrian claimant to the throne, who started a new dynasty in 1485

Henry VI Lancastrian king at the start of the Wars of the Roses, who suffered bouts of mental illness

John of Gaunt The powerful uncle of Richard II who ruled on his behalf

Margaret Beaufort The mother of Henry Tudor, who played a central role in his bid for the throne

Margaret of Anjou The French wife of Henry VI, who took charge of the House of Lancaster

Richard III The youngest brother of Edward IV, who seized the English throne from his nephews

Richard of York A wealthy nobleman who organised opposition to King Henry VI's reign

The Earl of Warwick A powerful nobleman who helped both Henry VI and Edward IV take the throne

Wat Tyler Leader of the Peasants' Revolt, thought to have been a yeoman from Kent

Origins of Islam

Between his first divine revelation in 610 CE and his death in 632 CE, Muhammad united the Arabian Peninsula under a new faith – **Islam.**

For centuries, **Bedouins** had roamed across the deserts of Arabia leading caravans of camels loaded with goods. Many **clans** had grown wealthy as guides for merchants bringing carpets and tapestries from Persia, spices from India, incense and perfumes from Arabia, silks and porcelain from China, and gold and ivory from East Africa. However, it remained a harsh landscape in which to make a living, and raids on rival tribes were a common way to survive.

A desert caravan of camels loaded with goods

By the 7th century CE, a permanent Arab settlement had emerged in **Mecca**. Here, the Bedouins worshipped a variety of **idols** from different faiths, held inside a shrine called the **Kaaba**.

The most powerful tribe who ruled over Mecca was the **Quraysh**. In 610 CE a member of the Quraysh named Muhammad had a vision that he was visited by the Archangel Jibril, who was sent from Allah (the Arabic name for God). Jibril told Muhammad that he was the final **Prophet**, following Adam, Abraham, Moses, Jesus and others. Muhammad was shocked and worried about these visions, but his first wife Khadija, a wealthy and successful trader herself, persuaded him to recite them. Muhammad called the words he had heard from Allah the Quran, meaning 'recitation'. They emphasised that there was only one God to be worshipped – Allah – and he was the final judge.

When people heard these words, many began to convert to Islam, meaning 'surrender to the will of God'. A **Muslim** became the term for someone who had made this surrender to Allah.

Religious similarities

Judaism, Christianity and Islam are all **monotheistic** religions based on belief in one God and their descent from the Prophet Abraham. Muhammad himself did not believe that he was beginning a new religion, but simply bringing monotheism to the pagan Arabs. As the Arabs conquered new territories, many customs from Judaism and Christianity were absorbed or continued, including the veiling and segregation of women in public. Mosques used domes like Christian Orthodox churches and Jewish synagogues. In addition, old Bedouin traditions were continued, such as walking around the Kaaba seven times during **hajj** (the pilgrimage to Mecca), to make the transition to Islam easier.

The golden 'Dome of the Rock' Islamic shrine and the dome of a Christian church in Jerusalem

The Quraysh were angry that Muhammad attacked their traditional customs, insulted their gods and forbade moneylending. His words threatened the Quraysh leadership of Mecca, so they branded Muhammad a liar and persecuted his followers. Together, Muhammad and his followers fled the city in 622 ce during a period known as the Hijrah ('migration'). They sought refuge in a town called Yathrib, which was populated by Arab and Jewish tribes who were generous people and shared their homes and belongings with the Muslim exiles. It was here that Muhammad learned more about the Jewish faith. In particular, he learned that Abraham had another son named Ismail, who had been sent into the Arabian desert to be the 'father of a great nation'. Muhammad saw Ismail as the ancestor of the Arab Muslims, and Yathrib was renamed Medina (short for 'the enlightened city') in honour of the Prophet Ismail.

The Quraysh in Mecca were still determined to destroy this new Islamic faith and sent an army towards Medina. In 624, at the Battle of Badr, Muhammad assembled the first Muslim army in history. His small force was victorious despite being heavily outnumbered by the Quraysh forces. Soon after, accusations arose that the Jewish tribes of Medina were plotting to betray Muhammad to the Quraysh and send him back to Mecca. After the Battle of Khandaq in 627, many of the Quraysh and Jewish tribes were defeated and Muhammad had over 600 men beheaded, seizing all of their goods and distributing them to his followers. Later, at the Battle of Hunayn, it is said Muhammad gained 24 000 camels and 6000 prisoners as loot. This continued to raise his profile as both a humble preacher but also a fearless warrior.

The return to Mecca

Many of the Bedouin tribes of Arabia joined Muhammad and converted to Islam, but the Quraysh refused to do so and maintained control of Mecca. When Muhammad dared to head towards Mecca unarmed to perform hajj, a tentative peace was established, but it was soon broken by the Quraysh.

Muslim pilgrims at the Kaaba in the Haram Mosque of Mecca, Saudi Arabia, during hajj

In 630, Muhammad returned to Mecca with 10 000 soldiers gathered from across Arabia. Abu Sufyan, leader of the Quraysh, realised that the only way to avoid conflict was to surrender and convert to Islam. He agreed to help Muhammad smash the hundreds of pagan idols kept inside the Kaaba and re-dedicated it to Allah. By the time of his death in 632, the Prophet Muhammad had successfully united most of the tribes of Arabia under the Islamic faith.

Check your understanding

1. What did the Bedouins help to trade across Arabia?
2. What was revealed by the Archangel Jibril in Muhammad's vision?
3. What did the Quryash tribe do to Muhammad in Mecca in 622 ce?
4. What happened after the Battle of Badr and the Battle of Khandaq?
5. How was Muhammad able to unite most of the tribes of Arabia?

Unit 6: The Islamic world
The caliphates

Following Muhammad's death in 632 CE, someone was needed to lead the Islamic faith. Deciding who this leader should be was not easy.

A single political and religious leader ruling the Islamic world was known as the **caliph**. In the following centuries, a succession of caliphs expanded the reach of Islam at a fast pace, establishing **caliphates** that stretched from Spain in the west to India in the east.

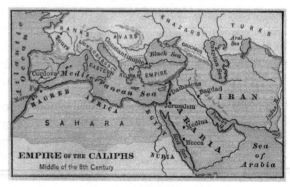

The extent of the empire of the Arab Caliphs in the middle of the 8th century (shaded pink)

The Rashidun, 632–661

The first caliph was Muhammad's father-in-law, Abu Bakr. He quelled Bedouin uprisings in Arabia, emphasising that it was forbidden for Muslims to fight each other. The second caliph, Umar, expanded the caliphate into Egypt, Syria and Iraq during his ten-year rule. With a growing army that reached 100 000, he gained control of these lands and built fortified towns to protect his gains.

In 644 Umar was stabbed in a Medina mosque by an enslaved Persian, and Uthman was elected as the third caliph. Uthman controversially decided to appoint Muawiya as governor of Syria. Muawiya was the son of Muhammad's old Quraysh enemy Abu Sufyan of Mecca, who had constantly battled Muhammad. Discontent rose among those who believed people from Medina who had helped the Prophet Mohammad were not being chosen for positions of power.

In 656 Uthman was assassinated and Muhammad's cousin Ali became the fourth caliph. Ali immediately opposed Muawiya, who refused to obey. A bitter five-year civil war began and a split in the Islamic community emerged. The **Shia** argued that Ali was the first legitimate caliph, as he was a blood relation to the Prophet Mohammad. However, the **Sunni** argued that the caliph did not need to be a direct descendent of Mohammad, and that the first four caliphs were the 'Rashidun' ('rightly guided').

The Umayyads, 661–750

To end the civil war in 661, Ali was stabbed with a poisoned sword while at prayer and died. Muawiya founded the **Umayyad** dynasty and established a strong centralised government from his power base in Syria, where he had been governor. He made **Damascus** the new capital of the Islamic world – a political move to link the caliphate with the Umayyads.

Under the Umayyads, Islamic power increased through invasion and conversion westwards to Libya, Algeria, Morocco and Spain, and eastwards to Afghanistan and

The Great Mosque of the Umayyads in Damascus, Syria – one of the largest and oldest mosques in the world

the borders of India. Arabic was established as the official language of the caliphate and new coinage was minted. The oldest examples of Islamic architecture were also built during this time, such as the **Dome of the Rock** in Jerusalem, completed in 692 CE.

Religious divisions between Sunni and Shia Muslims continued. At the Battle of Karbala in Iraq in 680 CE, Ali's son Husayn refused to submit to the Umayyads, and 72 supporters and family members, along with Husayn and his six-month-old son, were massacred.

The Abbasids, 750–1517

Calls by Shias for the caliphs to be blood descendants of Muhammad increased, and in 750 the **Abbasid** family staged a revolution and overthrew the Umayyads. The Abbasids were descended from Muhammad's uncle Abbas, and presented themselves as Shia while ruling as Sunni. However, they still faced opposition throughout their long reign.

The first Abbasid caliph, Abu al-Abbas, was said to have invited all the leading Umayyads to dinner then clubbed them to death. Abd al-Rahman was the only one to escape, fleeing to Spain and setting up a rival caliphate.

The second Abbasid caliph was Al-Mansur. He consolidated Abbasid rule into an absolute monarchy, called himself Al Mahdi ('the guided one') and claimed that Allah was giving him special help to rule. With the wealth he accumulated from conquests, parades and palaces became commonplace, giving a sense of majesty to the Abbasid rulers. In 762 he founded the great round city of **Baghdad** as the new capital of the caliphate. The diameter of the circular city was over 2 km with three rings of walls. At the centre lay his mosque complex and royal palace. The new city quickly became the centre of international trade and gained fame for its extensive libraries, such as the **Bayt al-Hikmah (House of Wisdom)**.

By 946, the Abbasids began to lose power. With such a vast empire, regional governors were given large amounts of independence and established their own dynastic power bases, paying only formal respect to the caliph in Baghdad. These new dynasties challenged the central power of the caliph and divided the Islamic world into many different states.

The Battle of Tours

By 732 CE, Umayyad forces had advanced as far as France, but their progress was stopped by the French prince Charles Martel at the Battle of Tours. While this was praised as a great victory for Christian Europe, the Arabs were not interested in the poor climate and limited wealth that could be gained from the remote kingdoms of northern Europe.

Aerial view of the walled city of Baghdad as it might have appeared in the 8th century, during the days of Al-Mansur

Check your understanding

1. Which empires did the new Arab caliphates gain territory from?
2. Why was Uthman's appointment of Muawiya as governor of Syria controversial?
3. What was the main religious division the caliphates faced?
4. How did the Abbasids seize power?
5. Which caliphate achieved the most success?

Islamic culture

The medieval Islamic world was a vibrant mixture of states stretching across three continents. It thrived on promoting new knowledge.

One of the key reasons for the rapid expansion of the caliphate following Muhammad's death was the fact that conquered peoples were not forced to convert to Islam. Non-Muslims in Muslim-held territory were required to pay a tax called the **jizya**. This tax showed submission to Muslim rule but allowed people to practise their own faith. The income that the jizya and other taxes generated for Muslim rulers enabled them to maintain cosmopolitan towns and cities, encouraging a great sharing of knowledge between different cultures.

The Ali Gholi Agha hammam (public bath) in Isfahan, Iran

Architecture and trade

Many Islamic cities had wonderful palaces and mosques decorated with intricate patterns and passages from the Quran. Mosque complexes had tall towers called minarets, from which a call to prayer would sound five times a day. Ritual washing was performed before daily prayers, and public baths known as hammams were built to ensure physical cleanliness. Irrigation (water) systems developed in Iran and Iraq were introduced to new territories to enable people to grow crops such as oranges, apricots and rice.

Islamic cities were huge: by 1000 CE, Baghdad is said to have had a population of over half a million, compared to about 20000 in London and Paris. **Souks** were full of luxurious goods from across the Islamic world. The caliphates grew rich in gold traded from African kingdoms such as Mali (see Unit 8) and a lucrative trade in enslaved people.

Learning and new discoveries

The Prophet Muhammad said that seeking knowledge was necessary for every Muslim. However, unlike Western Europe, where learning was kept in the hands of the Church, Islamic culture emphasised the pursuit of knowledge about the natural world as separate from religion. Some mosque complexes contained a **madrasa** (school) and library, allowing a wide spectrum of Muslims to become literate. These places of learning were open to both serious scholars and amateurs.

The Islamic world developed a deeper knowledge of astronomy, improving navigation instruments such as the astrolabe. Consequently, many stars have Arabic names. The Arab geographer al-Idrisi created the most accurate map yet available in Europe, showing areas as far away as Japan and Korea.

Ibn Battuta

The medieval world's most prolific traveller was a Moroccan named Ibn Battuta, who travelled some 116000 kilometres from West Africa to China. He dictated the stories of his adventures into a book, which became famous. Today, Ibn Battuta's stories reveal the extent of trade and diplomatic relations across the Islamic world.

Fact

In 859, Fatima al-Fihri set up the world's first university in Fez, Morocco – the University of al-Qarawiyyin. It continues to operate as a centre for higher education today.

In mathematics, a Persian Muslim named al-Khwarizmi developed new forms of algebra and popularised the numeral system that we still use today. Originally from India, it was Arab scholars who brought these numbers to the West as a more effective system than Roman numerals.

Advances in surgery such as anaesthetising patients with cannabis and opium, and using mercury and alcohol as antiseptics, helped people survive. Ibn Sina's *Canon of Medicine*, completed by 1025, remained a standard medical textbook for centuries, and al-Zahrawi wrote the first medical book to contain pictures of surgical tools and how to use them. With such advancements, an 11th-century Iraqi doctor was able to carry out the first known removal of a cataract from a patient's eye.

An astrolabe – a device for determining the coordinates and position of celestial objects

The House of Wisdom

Islamic rulers spent generously on education. The fifth Abbasid caliph, Harun al-Rashid, who ruled from 786 to 809, was a great supporter of scholarship, leading to a flourishing of learning and culture in Baghdad. He founded the Bayt al-Hikmah (House of Wisdom) as a library and centre for translating ancient Greek, Roman, Indian and Persian works, covering subjects such as science, philosophy, agriculture, geography, medicine, zoology and chemistry.

The Bayt al-Hikmah (House of Wisdom)

Arabs learned the secret of papermaking from prisoners taken after the Islamic victory at the Battle of Talas in 751, against the Chinese Tang dynasty. This meant that the libraries and scholarship of the Islamic world could flourish with a wider readership as books were cheaper to make with paper than vellum (animal skin) or papyrus used previously.

Check your understanding

1. How did the jizya tax help the Islamic caliphs?
2. What new types of architecture existed in Islamic cities?
3. Why was Islamic culture able to encourage the pursuit of knowledge?
4. What new discoveries were made by Islamic scholars?
5. Was the pursuit of knowledge the greatest achievement of the Islamic world?

Unit 6: The Islamic world
Islamic North Africa

As the popularity of Islam grew beyond the borders of Arabia, the territories of North Africa were an early area of expansion, from which the Fatimid caliphate emerged.

The extent of the Islamic conquests in North Africa stretched from Alexandria in Egypt to the Atlantic coastline of Morocco. This western empire became known as the **Maghreb** ('place where the sun sets').

Conversion of the Berbers

The Maghreb was inhabited by indigenous groups known to the Greeks and Romans as the **Berber** people. They had lived in this region since at least 10 000 BCE and were a mix of pagans, Christians and Jews. The Berbers were well known in the ancient world for being superb horse riders.

When the Umayyads began to invade North Africa, the Berbers resisted the encroaching Arab armies. Legend has it that the Berbers were led by a warrior queen named Dihya. At the Battle of Meskiana in 698, she inflicted such a devastating defeat on the Umayyad general Hasan that he fled to Libya for five years. Dihya used the Roman amphitheatre at El Djem (modern-day Tunisia) as a fortress and pursued a scorched earth policy of burning crops and resources to drive the Arabs out of the Maghreb. The Arabs were so astounded by Dihya's victories that they believed she could foresee the future and named her al-Kahina ('the priestess').

However, in 702 the Umayyads returned with a reinforced army and Dihya was killed in combat. Soon, the Berbers converted to Islam and adopted Arabic as one of their languages. The Berber Muslims were essential to the continued expansion of the Islamic empire into Iberia (Spain), with many Muslim generals and ruling dynasties coming from Berber backgrounds.

A traditional display of horsemanship in the Maghreb, today performed during festivals and to close wedding celebrations

Islamic Sicily

Sicily is a large island between North Africa and Italy, whose strategic position in the Mediterranean has been fought over throughout history. For centuries it had been ruled by the Byzantine empire, but in 827 a rebel Byzantine commander asked the Emir of Ifriqiya, Ziyadat Allah, to help him take control of the island. Seeing this as an opportunity to unite Arabs and Berbers in a shared conquest, Ziyadat sent 10 000 soldiers and 700 cavalrymen to conquer Sicily. By 902 the island's last Byzantine stronghold had fallen. Sicily remained under Muslim control until the Normans took control of the island in 1061.

In 909 a new dynasty was founded in Tunisia. The **Fatimids** were Shia Muslims, who claimed descent from the Prophet Muhammad's daughter Fatima. They began to wrest control of the Maghreb from the Abbasids, and by 969 they had conquered Egypt and established their own rival caliphate.

The Fatimids founded Cairo as the capital city of their rival caliphate, taking its name from the Arabic al-Qahirah meaning 'victorious'. Its position between the Mediterranean and Red Sea meant it became a huge international trading hub, amassing great riches. The Fatimid caliph Aziz, who ruled from 975 to 996, is said to have raised a ton of refined gold in taxation in just three days. The Fatimids encouraged the construction of buildings to rival the Abbasid capital in Baghdad. One Cairo palace of the Fatimid caliph was said to have 4000 rooms and 12 000 enslaved people and servants who provided him with all the goods and delicacies that he desired from across the Islamic world.

As a Shia dynasty, the Fatimids encouraged missionaries to travel throughout the Islamic world and convert Sunni Muslims. This meant that the Fatimids were a constant political and military threat to the Abbasids. Western European crusaders (see Unit 7) exploited these internal divisions within the Islamic world by employing either Fatimid or Abbasid mercenaries, depending on which Muslim-held lands they were trying to capture.

Minaret of the Al-Hakim Mosque in Cairo, Egypt, built in 992 CE

Despite this, as in the rest of the Islamic world, most Fatimid caliphs were tolerant of other religions and allowed non-Muslims to reach high office. One notable exception to this was the caliph Al-Hakim (996–1021), who destroyed the Christian Church of the Holy Sepulchre in Jerusalem and banned Christian pilgrims from visiting the city.

Mustansir was the eighth Fatimid caliph, and one of the longest reigning Muslim rulers of the Islamic world. He became caliph aged just 7 in 1036 and ruled until his death in 1094. However, during his reign there were several rebellions against Fatimid rule, and severe drought in about 1065–72 devastated Cairo.

The rising power of the Seljuk Turks and the sack of Jerusalem by the Western Europeans during the First Crusade in 1099 weakened the Fatimid caliphate further, reducing it to its Egyptian territories. The Fatimids were finally overthrown in 1171 by Salah al-Din, the great Muslim general who defeated the Third Crusade.

Bab al Futuh ('Conquest') Gate, in Cairo, Egypt, built during the reign of Caliph Mustansir, in 1087

Check your understanding

1. Who were the Berbers?
2. Why were the Arabs astounded by Dihya?
3. How did the Fatimids gain power?
4. Why was Cairo such a wealthy city?
5. Why did the Fatimid caliphate lose power?

Unit 6: The Islamic world
Islamic Spain

Having first invaded Spain in 711 CE, Muslim leaders ruled the Iberian Peninsula for centuries, until Christian armies reconquered their stronghold in Granada in 1492.

Since the collapse of the Roman Empire in the 5th century CE, Christian Germanic tribes known as the Visigoths had ruled Spain. However, by the 8th century their fragmented rule was easily crushed by the invading Muslim armies. The new land became known as **al-Andalus**.

In 750 the Abbasids overthrew and killed the Umayyads in Damascus, and Abd al-Rahman was the sole survivor of the Umayyad dynasty. He fled to al-Andalus and set up a rival caliphate, with Cordoba as its capital city. The Abbasids tried to stir up rebellions against the Umayyads in Al-Andalus, but Abd al-Rahman successfully put them down. In triumph, he sent a bag of rebel heads preserved in salt to Mecca for the Abbasid caliph al-Mansur who was performing his hajj (pilgrimage).

Moorish culture

The inhabitants of Islamic Spain were known as the **Moors** – people living in Islamic Iberia of mixed Arab, Berber and indigenous heritage. As with the rest of the Islamic world, non-Muslims were simply required to pay the jizya and could continue with their traditional customs. Jews flourished in places like Toledo, where previously the Visigoths had persecuted them. This ushered in a period known in Spain as the 'convivencia', when Christians, Jews and Muslims lived in harmony.

The cosmopolitan nature of Islamic Spain created a richly diverse Moorish culture with distinctive architecture and thriving centres of learning. Perhaps the most famous was **La Mezquita** in Cordoba – a huge mosque commissioned by Abd al-Rahman using 856 columns from old Roman buildings and distinctive red and white multi-tiered arches. It was said there were over 400 000 books in the library of Cordoba, and that the Umayyad caliphs spent a third of their income on funding such works.

Hypostyle Hall in the Mosque-Cathedral of Cordoba, Spain

The Reconquista

By 1032, the Umayyads of Cordoba had been weakened and political power was fragmenting among smaller, independent Muslim states known as **taifas**. The Christian kingdoms in northern Iberia saw this as an opportunity to start the **Reconquista** (reconquering) of the Iberian Peninsula.

In 1063 the Christian king Fernando I of Leon-Castille raided al-Andalus, forcing the taifas of Seville and Badajoz to pay him tribute. Thousands of gold dinars were sent to Fernando I and this money allowed him to strengthen and expand his army. Soon the Christian kingdoms had captured the strategically important city of Toledo, but the Berber

Almoravid dynasty stopped the Christian advance at the fiercely fought Battle of Sagrajas in 1086. The battleground became known as az-Zallaqah ('slippery ground') from the amount of blood spilled.

When Pope Urban II launched the First Crusade in 1095, a new enthusiasm for religious warfare in Western Europe was created, encouraging further attacks against the Iberian taifas. These conflicts continued for several centuries, made more complex by the rivalry between different taifas and Christian kingdoms.

The Reconquista cause was undermined by mercenary soldiers who fought for the Christian king or Islamic taifa, depending on who would pay them the most. The most legendary mercenary knight was Rodrigo Diaz de Vivar, better known by his Moorish name El Cid (from the Arabic 'sayyid' meaning 'lord'). El Cid commanded both Christian and Moorish armies, capturing Valencia from the Moors and carving out a kingdom for himself.

The success of Christian armies during the siege of Lisbon in 1147 established a new Christian Kingdom of Portugal in the west. After this, the power of the Berber Almohad dynasty of al-Andalus began to unravel after defeat at the Battle of Las Navas de Tolosa in 1212. Here, the Christian kings of Castille, Navarre and Aragon were able to put aside their differences and join forces. The great Islamic city of Cordoba fell to the Christians in 1236, followed by Seville in 1248.

Fact

Isabella became queen of Castile, age 23, in a coup against her brother. She enjoyed the strategic challenges of warfare – plotting campaigns, raising troops, negotiating alliances and even riding for days to personally intervene in disputes. She also took command of armour and artillery for the Spanish army.

However, there remained one Islamic territory in Spain that held out for another 200 years. The Nasrid dynasty ruled Granada from their magnificent hilltop fortress of the **Alhambra**, paying money to the northern Christian kings to maintain their existence. However, in 1469, when Isabella of Castille married Ferdinand II of Aragon, two powerful Christian kingdoms were united. They renewed military campaigns to once and for all complete the Reconquista. In 1492 Granada was besieged and Abu Abdallah Muhammad XII (known as Boabdil by the Christians) surrendered. Islamic rule in Spain was over.

The siege of Granada by the forces of Ferdinand II of Aragon and Isabella I of Castile, December 1491

The Spanish Inquisition

While Ferdinand and Isabella promoted the fall of Granada as 'liberation' from Muslim rule, their regime was much less religiously tolerant. They set up the Spanish Inquisition – a religious court whose aim was to root out people suspected of not being 'truly Catholic'. Jews and Muslims who had lived in Spain for centuries, including those who had already converted to Catholicism, were tortured and expelled to live elsewhere in Europe and North Africa.

Check your understanding

1. How were the Muslims able to conquer Iberia?

2. What did Abd al-Rahman do?

3. What was distinctive about Moorish culture?

4. Why was Fernando I's success in 1063 significant?

5. Why did the Reconquista take so long?

Knowledge organiser

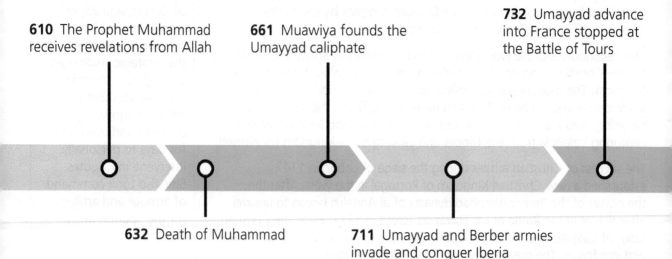

610 The Prophet Muhammad receives revelations from Allah

661 Muawiya founds the Umayyad caliphate

732 Umayyad advance into France stopped at the Battle of Tours

632 Death of Muhammad

711 Umayyad and Berber armies invade and conquer Iberia

Key vocabulary

Abbasids Caliphate established by al-Abbas in 750 CE

Al-Andalus Islamic name for Spain

Alhambra Hilltop fortress in Granada

Baghdad City in Iraq and the Abbasid capital

Bayt al-Hikmah (House of Wisdom) A great library founded by the Abassid caliph al-Mamun in Baghdad

Bedouins Nomadic people of Arabia

Berber Greco-Roman term for the indigenous people of North Africa

Caliph Single political and religious leader of an Islamic caliphate

Caliphate The land ruled by a caliph

Clans Close-knit group of people united by family relationships/common descent

Damascus City in Syria and the Umayyad capital

Dome of the Rock Islamic shrine where Muhammad is believed to have ascended to heaven

Fatimids Shia caliphate established in North Africa in 909 CE

Hajj Pilgrimage to Mecca

Iberian Peninsula Far south-western edge of Europe, which includes present-day Spain and Portugal

Idol Image or depiction of a god used as an object of worship

Islam A major world religion, begun by the Prophet Muhammad around 610 CE

Jizya Tax on non-Muslims living in Muslim lands

Kaaba Holy shrine in Mecca

La Mezquita Name of the Great Mosque of Cordoba, Spain

Madrasa School within a mosque complex

Maghreb Arabic word for North Africa, meaning 'the place where the sun sets'

Mecca Birthplace of the Prophet Muhammad and Islam's most important site of pilgrimage

Monotheistic Relating to a religion that worships one god

Moors People living in Islamic Iberia of mixed Arab, Berber and indigenous heritage

Muslim Person who follows Islam

Prophet Person regarded as an inspirational teacher proclaiming the will of God

Quraysh Powerful Arab tribe that ruled Mecca and exiled the prophet Muhammad from their clan

Reconquista Christian campaign to 'reconquer' Iberia from the Muslims that lasted many centuries

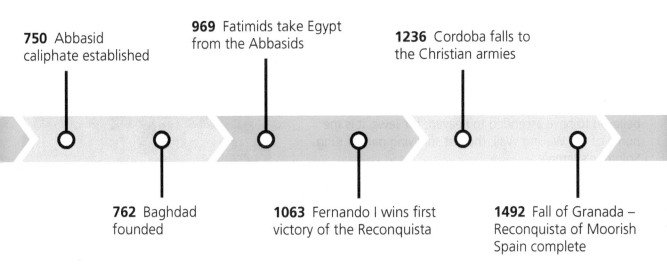

750 Abbasid caliphate established

969 Fatimids take Egypt from the Abbasids

1236 Cordoba falls to the Christian armies

762 Baghdad founded

1063 Fernando I wins first victory of the Reconquista

1492 Fall of Granada – Reconquista of Moorish Spain complete

Key people

Abd al-Rahman Last survivor of the Umayyad dynasty, who fled to Iberia and founded a rival caliphate in Cordoba

Abu al-Abbas Founder of the Abbasid dynasty that overthrew the Umayyads

Abu Sufyan Quraysh leader of Mecca who eventually surrendered to Muhammad in 630

Al-Mansur Abbasid caliph who founded the new city of Baghdad

Ali Fourth caliph of the Rashidun caliphate, who was ousted by Muawiya and killed; Shia Muslims believed his dynasty should have survived

Dihya Berber warrior queen who fought against the invading Arabs, also known as al-Kahina, 'the priestess'

Ferdinand II of Aragon and Isabella I of Castile King and Queen of Spain who completed the Reconquista and removed the last Muslim ruler from al-Andalus

Harun al Rashid Abbasid caliph who founded the House of Wisdom in Baghdad

Muawiya Governor of Syria, son of Abu Sufyan and founder of the Umayyad dynasty

Muhammad Prophet of the Islamic religion

Key vocabulary

Shia Muslim sect for whom the fourth caliph Ali was the first legitimate caliph after Muhammad's death

Souk Arab marketplace

Sunni Muslim sect that believe the first four 'Rashidun' caliphs were legitimate

Taifa Small Muslim states in Islamic Iberia from the 11th century onwards

Umayyads Caliphate established by Muawiya in 661

The First Crusade

The area surrounding the ancient city of **Jerusalem** is sometimes called the '**Holy Land**', and is a place of major religious importance for three world religions.

For Christians, Jerusalem is the home of the Church of the **Holy Sepulchre**, where Jesus is believed to have been buried and resurrected; for Muslims, it is the home of the Dome of the Rock, where the Prophet Muhammad is believed to have ascended to heaven; for Jews, it is the home of the Wailing Wall, the last surviving part of King Solomon's temple.

In 638 CE, Jerusalem was conquered by the expanding Islamic Empire. Jerusalem came to be ruled by the Fatimids, who tended to be tolerant of other religions, and for centuries they allowed Christians and Jews to live in the city, and visit as pilgrims. However, this changed by 1071, when a Muslim force known as the **Seljuk Turks** seized control of Jerusalem. The Seljuks, who were Sunni Muslims, originated from central Asia and were fierce warriors famed for their horseback archers. Christians feared that they were not welcome as pilgrims to Jerusalem now that it was under Seljuk rule, and could no longer visit the site of Jesus' resurrection.

Pope Urban II

More worrying still to the Christians, Seljuk power was extending through **Asia Minor** (modern-day Turkey) and threatening the Christian city of **Constantinople**, the capital of the **Byzantine Empire** (see Chapter 2, this unit). The Seljuk threat led the Byzantine Emperor Alexios Komnenos to ask for help from his Christian brothers in Western Europe. In response, Pope Urban II made one of the most important speeches in medieval history, on 27 November 1095.

In the French town of Clermont, Urban II addressed a gathering of important bishops and noblemen. He called on the knights of Europe to form a great army that would travel east, defend Constantinople, defeat the Seljuk Turks and conquer the Holy Land for the Christians. For those who took part, Urban II promised forgiveness of all previous sins and a guaranteed place in heaven. In doing so, he drew on a powerful idea: holy war. Ecstatic listeners who were inspired by Pope Urban II's call tore their clothing into crosses and sewed them onto their tunics. To fight in the **Crusades** became known as 'to take the cross'.

The Dome of the Rock, Jerusalem

The Wailing Wall, Jerusalem

The Church of the Holy Sepulchre, Jerusalem

The First Crusade

An army of perhaps 60 000 men, women and children was assembled from across Europe. It was the largest force Europe had seen since the days of the Roman Empire. Around one in ten were knights, the rest being a travelling city of foot soldiers, cooks, craftsmen, servants and family members.

This force was led by a group of noblemen from France, Germany and Italy. They included an ageing knight called Raymond of Toulouse, who claimed that his eye had been gouged out on a pilgrimage to Jerusalem, and Robert, Duke of Normandy, the eldest son of William the Conqueror. Another was Bohemond of Taranto, a giant of a man from Southern Italy and one of the most feared knights in Europe at the time.

In August 1096, the crusaders began their march into the unknown territory of Asia Minor, stopping beforehand at Constantinople where the Emperor Alexios Kommenos gave them food and supplies. In June 1097, they took the holy city Nicaea, and returned it to Byzantine rule. In June 1098, after an eight-month siege they captured the fortified city of Antioch. Marching through endless miles of hot, dry terrain towards the Holy Land, the crusaders quickly ran out of food and water, and survived by looting nearby villages.

> **Fact**
>
> During the long winter of 1098, starving crusaders trapped in the city of Antioch ate seeds from horse manure to survive. Crusaders in the nearby city of Maarat were said to have resorted to cannibalism.

Siege of Jerusalem

After three years and 3000 gruelling miles, the crusaders finally reached Jerusalem, on 7 June 1099. Starvation, casualties and desertion had depleted their army to 15 000 men and 1300 knights. They camped outside the walls of Jerusalem for a month to regain their strength and build siege engines. One knight, named Godfrey of Bouillon, built a 20-metre-tall siege tower. Godfrey took his tower to the less defended northern walls of the city, and on 15 July he broke through the Muslim defences. The crusaders flooded into the city.

Once inside Jerusalem, the crusaders massacred the Muslim and Jewish population, killing, torturing and burning alive an estimated 10 000 men, women and children. It was reported that blood ran through the streets up to their ankles, and six months later the city still reeked of death and decay. This butchery by the crusader knights shocked the Islamic world.

Modern illustration of the siege of Jerusalem

Check your understanding

1. Why is Jerusalem a place of major importance for three world religions?
2. What did the Pope promise to Christian knights who agreed to take part in the First Crusade?
3. Who led the First Crusade?
4. Why did the crusaders resort to looting as they made their way towards Jerusalem?
5. How did the crusaders behave once they had broken into Jerusalem?

The Second Crusade

During their progress through the Holy Land, the crusaders established a network of 'crusader states' ruled by European knights. However, the survival of such states was far from certain.

Following the Siege of Jerusalem, Godfrey of Bouillon took control of the city. He refused to be crowned 'King of Jerusalem', believing that only Jesus Christ could wear such a crown. However, when Godfrey died one year later in 1100, his power-hungry brother was crowned King Baldwin I of Jerusalem.

The city of Antioch had historically been ruled by the crusaders' allies, the Byzantines (see box). The crusaders had sworn an oath to return Antioch to the Byzantine Emperor if they took it from Muslim rule. Instead, Bohemond of Taranto made himself Prince of Antioch, leading to tension between the crusaders and their Byzantine allies.

Krak des Chevaliers, a crusader castle in Syria

Other crusader states included the County of Tripoli north of Jerusalem, and the County of Edessa in modern-day Turkey. From these cities, crusader knights expanded their power into the surrounding countryside, where they built castles to establish control over new territories, such as the enormous Krak des Chevaliers in Syria. Along the Mediterranean coastline, they captured port towns such as **Acre** (taken in 1104) and Tripoli (taken in 1109). In addition to the wealth gained from these major coastal cities, this ensured that a steady supply of reinforcements and pilgrims could travel from Western Europe to the Holy Land.

Byzantine Empire

Situated between the Islamic world and Christian Europe was a civilisation known as the Byzantine Empire. The Roman Empire divided during the 4th Century CE, with Rome as the capital of the western half and Byzantium (later Constantinople) as the capital of the eastern half. After the fall of Rome in 476, the Byzantine Empire survived for another 1000 years. The Byzantines called themselves 'Romans', spoke Greek, and had as their capital the walled city of Constantinople (modern-day Istanbul). They were Christians, but belonged to the **Eastern Orthodox Church**, which meant their alliances with crusaders were always uneasy.

The church of Hagia Sofia in Constantinople (modern-day Istanbul, in Turkey)

European visitors to Constantinople during the Crusades spoke of its magnificent buildings. Most spectacular of all was the church of **Hagia Sofia**, which remained the largest cathedral in the world for 1000 years after it was built. When the French crusader knight Geoffrey of Villehardouin laid eyes on Constantinople during the Fourth Crusade, he recorded he "never thought that there could be so rich and powerful a place on Earth".

The Second Crusade

One reason for the extraordinary success of the First Crusade was the infighting between different Muslim leaders in the Middle East, but this began to change during the 1100s. Imad al-Din **Zengi**, was a Muslim ruler from Mosul (modern-day Iraq) who hoped to build a unified kingdom across modern day Syria and the surrounding area. He criticised the Muslim leaders who made alliances with the crusader states, and along with his son Nur al-Din, inspired Muslim leaders to unite against Christian invaders. In doing, Zengi and his successors began an Islamic holy war of their own, a '**Jihad**' in Arabic.

In 1144, Zengi's forces captured the crusader state of Edessa. A newly elected Pope named Eugenius III called upon the knights of Europe to embark on a Second Crusade and retake the land. This inspired two European kings, Louis VII of France and Conrad III of Germany, who took the cross and assembled a force of 50 000 men. Eleanor of Aquitaine (see Unit 4, Chapter 5) also went on this crusade and her involvement inspired other nobles to join.

However, Louis and Conrad were not successful leaders. Despite advice to the contrary, they travelled overland to Jerusalem, which greatly weakened their forces. Once in the Holy Land, Louis and Conrad made no attempt to retake Edessa, as much of the city had been destroyed in another attack in 1146. Instead, the two kings chose to attack the far larger and wealthier city of Damascus, famed for its abundant fruit orchards, expensive fabrics, and swords made of the famous Damascene steel. However, the Siege of Damascus in 1148 lasted just five days before the crusader army withdrew. The two Kings Louis and Conrad returned to Europe humiliated.

Fact

Two years after he took Edessa, Zengi was assassinated by Yarankash, an enslaved man who served him, who was allegedly furious with Zengi for scolding him after he drank from Zengi's goblet.

Melisende, Queen of Jerusalem

Before he died in 1131, King Baldwin II of Jerusalem decreed that his spirited daughter Melisende would rule Jerusalem as a joint monarch with her husband, and her son. Both tried to sideline Melisende, but she resisted, remaining a significant figure in Jerusalem politics right until her death in 1161. During the reigns of her father, husband and son, she conducted alliances, built Christian convents, and commissioned the Melisende Psalter – a prayer book that remains one of the most valuable examples of crusader art today.

The Presentation of Christ in the Temple from the Psalter of Queen Melisende

Check your understanding

1. What were the 'crusader states', and how many of them were established?
2. Why did the crusaders and the Byzantine Empire have an uneasy alliance?
3. Why was Queen Melisende a significant figure in the Kingdom of Jerusalem?
4. What caused the Second Crusade?
5. Why did the Second Crusade damage the reputation of European crusaders?

Unit 7: The Crusades
The Third Crusade

The capture of Jerusalem in 1187 led to the Third Crusade, and a showdown between two of the greatest commanders of the medieval world: Salah al-Din and Richard the Lionheart.

Salah al-Din was the son of a Kurdish general in Zengi's army, who grew up to be a great military leader. He became **Sultan** of Egypt in 1174, and from there he began his single-minded campaign to unite the lands of Egypt, Palestine, Syria and Iraq under his rule. In the summer of 1187, his army set up camp beside the Sea of Galilee, 100 miles from Jerusalem, intent on expelling the Christian occupiers from the Holy City.

The King of Jerusalem, Guy of Lusigan, decided to attack Salah-al-Din's camp with his entire army, despite the summer heat and lack of water on Galilee's plains. The ensuing Battle of Hattin was a catastrophe. Salah-al-Din's army surrounded the crusader knights, setting fire to the scrubland so their already parched throats choked on the smoke. Salah al-Din captured most of Guy's army and beheaded 200 of his knights. Guy was imprisoned in Damascus, and three months later Salah al-Din took Jerusalem. Over the next two years, Salah al-Din captured 50 more crusader strongholds, including the port city of Acre.

Statue of Richard the Lionheart outside the Houses Of Parliament in Westminster, London, England

The Archbishop of Tyre sailed to Rome with news of Jerusalem's fall, in a boat with sails depicting Salah al-Din's horses stabled in the Church of the Holy Sepulchre. It was said that, on hearing the news, Pope Urban III died of shock. The new Pope Gregory VIII had little option but to call for a Third Crusade. Three of Europe's most powerful kings took the cross: King Richard I of England (known as the 'Lionheart'), Emperor Frederick Barbarossa of Germany (meaning 'red beard') and King Philip II of France.

At 68 years old, Barbarossa was an experienced military leader with a large army, but he drowned at a river crossing in Anatolia before reaching the Holy Land. This left the English and French kings in command, but they were bitter rivals, and Philip bore a grudge against Richard in part for refusing to marry his sister. Richard I conquered Cyprus on the way to the Holy Land and arrived in June 1191. Here, he found King Philip, the remainder of the German army, and the survivors of the Battle of Hattin laying siege to Acre.

Richard seized control of the siege from Philip and forced Salah al-Din to surrender Acre on 12 July 1191. When Duke Leopold, the commander of the remaining German knights, placed his banner on the walls of Acre, Richard took it down, furious that Leopold was taking credit for his success. Richard was unforgiving in victory: as part of the peace negotiations, Salah al-Din promised to return to the crusaders a relic believed to be part of the cross of Christ, which had been captured

Fact

Richard the Lionheart decided to conquer Cyprus after his sister and fiancée were shipwrecked on the island and imprisoned by its Byzantine ruler Isaac Komnenos. Richard imprisoned Isaac, freed his fiancée, and married her on the island.

at Hattin. Salah al-Din delayed in fulfilling the agreement. So, Richard marched 2700 Muslim soldiers outside of Acre's city walls and executed them in full sight of Salah al-Din and his army.

Following the Siege of Acre, Philip returned to France, and Richard took full command of the crusader forces. He defeated Salah al-Din's forces again at the Battle of Arsuf, and steadily progressed towards Jerusalem. By January 1192, Richard was just 12 miles from the city. However, by this point he was ill, his soldiers exhausted, and the weather was dreadful. Doubting his ability to take the city, Richard decided to turn back towards Acre.

The fortified coastal city of Acre, in modern-day Israel

Although fierce rivals, Richard and Salah al-Din grew to respect each other's military ability, and their exhausted armies agreed to a truce in the summer of 1192. Jerusalem remained in Muslim hands, but the crusaders were allowed to keep the valuable strip of coastal land around Acre. In addition, Christians were given full permission to visit Jerusalem on pilgrimage.

Salah al-Din the Merciful

Although Salah al-Din was a fierce warrior, he was respected for showing mercy towards his enemies. Having conquered Jerusalem, Salah al-Din ordered that his men should not kill civilians or loot their possessions. Enemy knights were given the chance to buy their freedom, or be sold as enslaved people. During a battle at Jaffa, Richard the Lionheart's horse was killed beneath him, and Salah al-Din was said to have responded by sending him a new horse. When Richard was suffering from a terrible fever during the summer of 1192, Salah al-Din sent him peaches and sherbet cooled with snow from nearby mountains to help him recover. Salah al-Din intended to visit **Mecca** on a pilgrimage at the end of the Third Crusade, but he died of a fever in 1193.

Statue of Salah al-Din

Check your understanding

1. Who was Salah al-Din, and what was his ambition?
2. What was the outcome of the Battle of Hattin in 1187?
3. How did Christian Europe respond to the news of the Battle of Hattin?
4. Did the Third Crusade end in victory for Salah al-Din or Richard the Lionheart?
5. Does Salah al-Din deserve to be remembered as 'the Merciful'?

Life as a crusader knight

By promising knights that crusading would allow them to fight and kill, but still be rewarded with eternity in heaven, Pope Urban II created a powerful new movement in Christianity.

Religious language and imagery were constantly used to recruit knights for the Crusades. Preachers such as the monk Bernard of Clairvaux travelled Europe whipping crowds into a religious frenzy. He told them "The Earth trembles and is shaken because the King of Heaven has lost his land, the land where once he walked."

However, religion was not the sole motivation. As the crusader states grew, some knights saw the Crusades as an opportunity to gain fame. Stories of great crusader knights, such as Godfrey of Bouillon and Richard the Lionheart, inspired other knights to seek glory in the Holy Land. For peasants, crusades offered the chance to escape grinding poverty and the control of their feudal overlords.

Fighting a Crusade

Going on a Crusade was expensive. A knight had to pay for himself, and also for weapons, armour, equipment and food, not to mention a small entourage of foot soldiers and servants. One historian estimates that going on crusade cost four times the annual income of a poor knight.

Very few knights would return home from a crusade wealthier than when they left. That is, if they returned home at all. The survival rate for crusaders was not good. One in three of the knights who left for the First Crusade died, through battle, starvation or disease. Hunger was a constant companion for crusaders, who often had to resort to eating horses, dogs and rats to survive.

Once knights reached the Holy Land, they faced diseases such as dysentery, malaria and cholera. The weather was another problem: the scorching heat of the summer reached unbearable temperatures for knights in a European suit of armour, while rain and snow caused armour to rust during the winter.

If taken prisoner following a battle, crusader knights could expect to be beheaded or enslaved. Knights also lived in fear of a sect of strict Shia Muslims who lived in the Syrian mountains and carried out surprise killings. Their chosen weapon was a dagger, and they smoked hashish to bolster their courage, giving birth to their name – the **Assassins**.

Life in the Holy Land

For knights who settled in the crusader kingdoms, life could be pleasant. European settlers often adopted the lifestyles of eastern Muslims, who they called '**Saracens**' (an old Greek word and Latin word for people living

> ### Fact
>
> After Salah al-Din conquered Jerusalem in 1187, settlers in the East sent their Christian brothers in Europe a picture of a Muslim warrior, whose horse was defecating on the Holy Sepulchre.

Window depicting a Knight Templar

in Arabia). They washed regularly, ate Middle Eastern food, and wore turbans. Arabic houses, with courtyards, fountains and glass windows, were far more luxurious than their draughty castles back home in Europe.

Fulcher of Chartres, the priest to King Baldwin I of Jerusalem, recorded that European settlers in the Holy Land married local women and adopted local languages. He wrote, "We who were westerners have now been made easterners. He who was a Roman or a Frank is now a Galilaean, or an inhabitant of Palestine…."

Many European women settled in the Holy Land, often as the wives of crusader knights or as nuns establishing new holy orders. As the rulers of crusader states frequently died defending their lands, it was not uncommon for their widows or daughters – such as Queen Melisende of Jerusalem – to gain political power. Some female crusaders even fought in battle. However, the number of European women on the battlefield may have been exaggerated by Muslim accounts, to discredit their Christian foe.

A bewildering array of different races and religions lived in the Holy Land: Armenians, Greeks, Arabs and Jews. However, European settlers ruled over them all, imposing European-style systems of feudal government. There was some interaction between the Christians and Muslims, particularly through trade, but the majority of Muslims were forced to live as peasants.

Military orders

During the Crusades, a new concept within Christianity developed: the warrior-monk. These were religious orders that lived together, and took vows of poverty, chastity and obedience. However, they were also fighters, feared for their discipline and devotion.

One of the best known were the **Knights Templar**, who were formed in 1120 to protect Christian pilgrims to the Holy Land, and were given a royal palace at the al-Aqsa mosque on Temple Mount in Jerusalem. The Templars answered to no king, but instead elected a 'Grand Master'. The Templars grew long beards, held initiation ceremonies, and were not allowed to leave the field of battle while the Templar banner remained standing. Due to their great popularity, the Templars were granted a number of castles and territories to rule and became very wealthy. Others grew jealous and suspicious of their power. In 1312 the Pope ordered the Templars to disband.

Another elite order of crusader knights was the **Knights Hospitaller**. After crusaders were driven from the Holy Land, the Knights Hospitaller moved to Cyprus, then Rhodes, and continued as a religious and military order on the island of Malta until 1798.

> ### Fact
> Love affairs between Christians and Muslims could be cruelly punished in crusader states: according to a law established in 1120, women would have their nose cut off, and men would be castrated.

Window depicting a Knight Hospitaller

Check your understanding

1. How much has one historian estimated it cost a poor knight to go on crusade?

2. Why was the armour of European knights unsuited to fighting in a crusade?

3. In what ways did European crusaders adopt 'Eastern' ways once they settled in the Holy Land?

4. What was the social status of Muslims living under Christian rule in the Holy Land?

5. What were the Knights Templar and Knights Hospitaller?

The end of the Crusades

Fewer than 10 years had passed since Richard the Lionheart's retreat from Jerusalem, before Pope Innocent III was calling for yet another crusade.

In 1201, the great maritime republic of Venice was asked to construct a fleet of 200 ships for a fourth crusade, but by June 1202 the crusader force had still not raised the money to pay for them. However, a solution was at hand. A Byzantine prince named Alexios Angelos was living in exile in Europe, after his uncle had blinded his father and seized Constantinople. Alexios asked the crusaders to help him take back his father's throne. In return, Alexios promised to pay the crusaders the money they required to complete their journey to the Holy Land.

The Fourth Crusade

In April 1203, the crusaders set sail for Constantinople. They broke through the supposedly impenetrable sea walls of Constantinople using ships fitted with specially designed siege towers, and took the city. Alexios was proclaimed Emperor.

However, once made Emperor, Alexios was unable to raise the money he promised the crusaders, and relations grew bitter. In early 1204, Alexios was overthrown by his own people and strangled to death. With Alexios dead, 20 000 impatient crusaders were left camping outside Constantinople with no chance of gaining the money they had been promised. So, they took Constantinople by force.

Surviving portion of the walls of Constantinople, in modern-day Istanbul, Turkey

In April 1204, the crusaders broke into Constantinople, subjecting its population to three days of violence and plunder. The greatest Christian city on earth was destroyed, stripped of its treasures and relics, including what were believed to be Jesus' crown of thorns and the head of John the Baptist. Happy with their plunder, the crusaders decided not to bother carrying on to Jerusalem, and sailed home to Western Europe.

The end of the Crusades

There were further Crusades during the 13th century, often focused on taking the Muslim power base of Egypt before progressing to Jerusalem. However, the concept of 'crusading' had changed. It was increasingly used to justify wars against non-Christians, not just in the Holy Land but across Europe and North Africa.

> ### Fact
> It is believed that in 1212, thousands of youngsters left their families in France and Germany and embarked on what became known as the 'Children's Crusade'. Accounts suggest the youngsters set sail for the Holy Land, but were captured and enslaved in North Africa.

The **Mamluks** were originally enslaved-soldiers from central Asia. They gained enough military strength to overpower their Arab rulers, and took control of Egypt. In the face of Mamluk attack, some of the Christian population escaped by sea, others were enslaved. At first, the Mamluks promised to treat captured crusader knights from the Hospitaller and Templar orders with mercy, but then took them outside Acre's city walls to be executed.'

Impact of the Crusades

The Crusades transformed life in Europe. Pilgrims from Europe arrived in the Holy Land by the boatload to see Biblical history with their own eyes: Bethlehem, Nazareth, Galilee and the River Jordan.

Visiting Europeans learned from the cultural and intellectual wealth of the Islamic world. Soap, mirrors and magnifying glass all came to Europe via the Islamic world, as did modern numerals (1,2, 3…) and algebra, which comes from the Arabic word 'al-jebr'. A stringed instrument called the lute and the board game chess also came to Europe from the Middle East, as did many texts from Ancient Greece and Rome that had been translated into Arabic.

Today, Christian pilgrims still travel to the River Jordan in the Holy Land to be baptised

Despite the fighting between Christian and Muslim armies, trade between Europe and the Middle East thrived during the Crusades. Italian city states, such as Venice and Genoa, grew extremely wealthy and established their own quarters in the coastal ports of Tripoli and Acre. Through these ports, goods were traded from as far afield as India and China. Sugar cane, olive oil, lemons, apricots and dates all became popular in Europe. Even Salah al-Din forged close trading links with Italians from Pisa, who sold him European timber to build his ships.

Due to the Crusades, Jews who had lived among Christians in Europe for centuries were increasingly attacked for being enemies of Christ, similar to Muslims. As knights marched through France and Germany to the First Crusade, they massacred thousands of Jews in the Rhineland. Because of rising levels of **anti-Semitism**, Jewish people were expelled from Germany during the 1100s, England in 1290, and France in 1306. The Crusades had given birth to a harder, more intolerant form of Christianity in Europe.

Check your understanding

1. What deal did the crusaders strike with the Byzantine prince Alexios during the Fourth Crusade?
2. Why did the crusaders turn against Alexios and sack Constantinople in 1204?
3. What event marked the end of the Crusades, and when did it take place?
4. What ideas and technologies did crusaders bring back to Europe from the Islamic world?
5. What effect did the Crusades have on the lives of Jews living in Europe?

Unit 7: The Crusades
Knowledge organiser

1095 Pope Urban II launches the First Crusade

1148 The Second Crusade ends in defeat after a failed attack on the city of Damascus

1192 The Third Crusade ends with peace between Richard I and Salah al-Din

1071 Seljuk Turks seize control of Jerusalem from the Fatimids

1099 Crusaders capture Jerusalem, creating the Kingdom of Jerusalem

1187 Salah al-Din captures Jerusalem, having defeated the crusader force at the Battle of Hattin

Key vocabulary

Acre Important crusader port city, and the crusaders' last stronghold in the Holy Land

Anti-Semitism The prejudice against and persecution of Jews as an ethnic group

Asia Minor A peninsula with the Mediterranean Sea to the south and the Black Sea to the north

Assassins Muslim sect that lived in the Syrian mountains and carried out surprise killings

Byzantine Empire A Greek-speaking offshoot of the Roman Empire, with Constantinople as its capital city

Constantinople The capital of the Byzantine Empire, and modern-day Istanbul

Crusade A religiously inspired war; the word comes from the Latin 'crux' meaning 'cross'

Crusader state New feudal states that were created in the Holy Land by European knights

Eastern Orthodox Church Eastern form of Christianity, followed by the Byzantines

Hagia Sofia Eastern Orthodox church in Constantinople, once the largest cathedral in the world

Holy Land An area of religious significance for three faiths on the Mediterranean's eastern shore

Holy Sepulchre Site of Christian pilgrimage, where the body of Jesus Christ is believed to be buried

Jerusalem Historic city, of major religious importance for Christianity, Islam and Judaism

Jihad An Islamic term meaning 'struggle', often used to describe a holy war

Knights Hospitaller An elite order of crusader knights, originally formed to run a hospital for pilgrims

Knights Templar An elite order of crusader knights, named after the Temple Mount in Jerusalem

Mamluks An Islamic dynasty formed by slave-soldiers that conquered Acre in 1291

Mecca Birthplace of the Prophet Muhammad and Islam's most important site of pilgrimage

Saracen Term used by crusaders to describe Muslim soldiers, taken from the Greek word for Arab

Seljuk Turks A Sunni Muslim tribe who conquered Jerusalem in 1079

Sultan The Arabic title for a ruler or emperor

1212 The so-called 'Children's Crusade' is thought to have left Europe for the Holy Land

1204 The Fourth Crusade ends with the sacking of Constantinople

1291 The last crusader stronghold of Acre falls to Mamluk invaders, ending the Crusades

Key people

Alexios Angelos Byzantine Emperor who invited the Fourth Crusade to invade Constantinople

Baldwin I The first Christian King of Jerusalem

Godfrey of Bouillon Crusader knight who led the siege of Jerusalem and became its first Christian ruler

Guy of Lusignan French knight, and King of Jerusalem at the time of the Third Crusade

Melisende Queen of Jerusalem who wielded power during the reigns of her husband and son

Prophet Muhammad A merchant from Mecca, who founded the Islamic religion

Richard I English king and brother of King John, known as 'the Lionheart'

Salah al-Din Muslim warrior, who captured Jerusalem from the crusaders in 1187

Urban II The Pope who began the First Crusade with a speech in Clermont

Zengi Muslim leader whose capture of Edessa prompted the Second Crusade

Unit 8: Medieval African kingdoms
Kingdoms of Aksum and Abyssinia

The **Kingdom of Aksum** was one of the earliest unified states in medieval Africa, and one of the first nations in the world to adopt Christianity as a state religion.

The Kingdom of Aksum traces its origins to the 1st century CE and covered the regions of modern Ethiopia, Eritrea, Sudan, Djibouti and Somalia in north-east Africa. It grew immensely powerful and rich by controlling trade routes to the Mediterranean through the Red Sea from China, India and Arabia as well as the rest of Africa.

In 327 CE, King Ezana I of Aksum officially adopted Christianity as his state religion. Tradition has it that a Christian missionary from the Holy Land named Frumentius was shipwrecked and enslaved in Ethiopia and forced to work as a tutor to the young Ezana. Frumentius converted Ezana to Christianity and became the first Bishop of Ethiopia – he is still known as 'abuna' ('our father') today.

> **Fact**
>
> In the 4th century, Aksum became the first sub-Saharan African state to mint its own coinage.

Trade and architecture

The Aksumite kings were patrons of the arts and Christianity. They financed the construction of churches and monasteries as well as translations of the Bible using a unique script called **Ge'ez** (pronounced geh-urrz). Related to Arabic and Hebrew, this script is still in use in Ethiopia today.

The Kingdom of Aksum had access to lucrative goods from other parts of Africa such as ivory from elephant tusks and rhino horns, as well as gold and emeralds. The Byzantine emperors were very keen on these objects as status symbols which drove the demand for the trade. In exchange, Aksum received goods such as wine and olive oil transported in terracotta amphorae, as well as textiles, glass vessels and beads, and iron and bronze weapons and lamps.

The Obelisk of Axum in northern Ethiopia, built in the 4th century CE

At the remains of the capital city of Aksum in northern Ethiopia, more than 100 granite **obelisks** have been found. They were probably used as tomb markers for members of the royal family and were carved with false doors and windows. The tallest would have stood 33 metres high and weighed 520 tonnes, making it the tallest obelisk in history. Remains of the palace in Aksum show stone lion-head gargoyles as decoration for roof drainage as well as plinths for metal statues, perhaps of kings or traditional gods before the adoption of Christianity.

With the rise of Islam in Arabia, the Kingdom of Aksum began to see increased competition for trade networks in the Red Sea. During the 10th century, the Kingdom of Aksum suffered rebellions and was overthrown by the Zagwe dynasty. These rulers held power for 300 years, ordering the construction of intriguing rock-cut churches such as those at Lalibela. But there were always anti-Zagwe factions, and the city of Aksum never lost its religious significance.

Solomonic Abyssinia

In 1270, the Kingdom of Aksum's former lands were consolidated by a new dynasty that claimed descent from the **House of Solomon**. Their first ruler, Yekuno-Amlak, was from Amhara (near modern Addis Ababa, Ethiopia), which became the capital of a new kingdom, **Abyssinia**. He traced his origins to 950 BCE, claiming that the Jewish King Solomon of Jerusalem and Queen Makeda of Sheba had a son called Menelik who travelled to Ethiopia carrying the **Ark of the Covenant**. This was the box said to contain the stone tablets of the Ten Commandments given to Moses. Although it is forbidden to view the artefact, it is believed that the Church of Maryam Tsion in northern Ethiopia still holds the Ark of the Covenant to this day.

Church of Saint Mary of Zion, where the Ark of the Covenant is allegedly kept

Abyssinian kingship was legitimised by descent from the House of Solomon and through possession of the Ark of the Covenant. To promote their Christian credentials, Abyssinian kings sent letters and embassies to various cities in the Mediterranean, often to seek holy relics to adorn their churches. Abyssinian pilgrims frequently travelled to Jerusalem but did not involve themselves in the European crusades of the medieval period.

Debre Birhan Selassie Church in Gondar, Ethiopia, built in the 17th century

During the reign of Amda Seyon I, in 1314–44, the Abyssinian Empire doubled in size. The Solomonic kings used various strategies to control their new territories. Non-Christian rulers who had previously been independent would remain in power, but their children had to live as courtiers at the Solomonic court to ensure loyalty. Civil wars were prevented by confining all male relatives except sons of the king within monasteries. The king also used land grants known as **gults** to encourage people from the central loyal areas of Solomonic control to settle in the more distant regions of the empire. Those who received a gult were allowed to extract their own personal tribute from local farmers.

> ### Fact
> The Solomonic dynasty remained in power in Ethiopia until 1974 when the last emperor of Ethiopia, Haile Selassie, was deposed by a military coup and died.

Check your understanding

1. Which modern countries did the Kingdom of Aksum have control over?
2. Why did King Ezana I convert the Kingdom of Aksum to Christianity?
3. What did the Kingdom of Aksum trade?
4. Who did Yekuno-Amlak claim descent from?
5. How did the Solomonic dynasty maintain their authority?

Kingdom of Mali

During the 13th century, the **Kingdom of Mali** grew wealthy from controlling the trans-Saharan trade route. Fame of its riches spread through Europe and Asia.

In the medieval world, West Africa was known to Arabic scholars as the 'land of gold'. Camel loads of the precious metal were transported across the Sahara Desert and traded in North Africa. From there, the gold would be used to mint coins and adorn mosques and palaces throughout the Islamic world, as well as churches in Christian Europe.

The **Kingdom of Ghana** (in modern-day Mauritania) was one of the first kingdoms to use its prime location to dominate this trade in gold. Ghana's rulers grew powerful and rich from taxing these imports and exports. Contact with the Islamic world also meant that many merchant families converted to Islam, and Arabic became the language of commerce and administration.

Rise of Mali

During the 13th century, a new leading power emerged in West Africa under a man named Sundiata. Born unable to walk, Sundiata's disability did not hinder his power to unite the chiefdoms around the Upper Niger River and establish the Mali Empire. In 1235, Sundiata was crowned **Mansa**, meaning 'king of kings'. As Mansa, he expanded Mali's control of the gold fields from modern Senegal and Guinea in the east to Ghana and the Cote d'Ivoire in the south.

Sundiata guaranteed that chiefs from each conquered area were represented in the **gbara** (assembly). This ensured that everyone in the Mansa's empire adhered to his decisions, but also acted as a check on his power. The establishment of the gbara was laid out by Sundiata in the **Kurukan Fuga**, a charter outlining the laws his people would follow. The charter also advocated how others should be treated with women involved in all levels of decision making.

The Mansa displayed his authority by sitting on an ebony throne with elephant tusks on each side and holding a bow and quiver of arrows. A silk parasol was held over his head, and he spoke only through a **jeli** (an oral historian who served the Mansa). If non-Muslims wanted to address the Mansa, they had to sprinkle dust on their heads and fall to their hands and knees. He wore a golden headdress and a red robe. Drums, elephant tusk trumpets and rosewood xylophones would announce his arrival, surrounded by an honour guard of 300 soldiers.

Mansa Musa

From 1312, **Mansa Musa** ruled the Mali empire after the previous emperor left for an expedition across the Atlantic Ocean, and never returned. During the 25 years of Mansa Musa's reign, Mali experienced a golden age.

Fact

In 1154 the Islamic geographer al Idrisi described a gold nugget in the ruler of Ghana's palace that was so large he tied his horse to it.

Oral history

Oral history is a source of information about the past found in the stories passed down through the generations. Written records are rarer from the African kingdoms compared to Europe, China or the Islamic world, which means that oral history is particularly important. Both the Epic of Sundiata and the Kurukan Fuga are known to us thanks to these oral histories.

In 1324, Mansa Musa left Mali to go on hajj (the pilgrimage to Mecca). This was a vast journey of at least 3000 miles, involving crossing the Sahara Desert where entire caravans could get lost or perish in a sandstorm. Travelling with his senior wife Inari Kunate, Mansa Musa took with him court officials, soldiers, servants and enslaved people totalling up to 60 000 people, and 80 camel loads of gold.

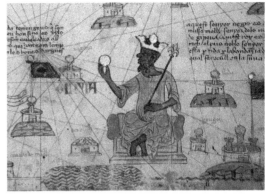

Although Mansa Musa was not the first West African ruler to make hajj, the huge scale of his procession left a deep impression on those he met. When he arrived in Cairo in July 1324, it is said he gave out so much gold that there was a crash in the price of gold across Europe. Mansa Musa became known as the richest individual in the entire Medieval world.

Returning to Mali, Mansa Musa brought with him Muslim scholars and architects to help strengthen Islam within his kingdom. The cities of Gao, Djenne and **Timbuktu** became great centres of learning with mosque complexes complete

Mansa Musa sitting on a throne and holding a gold coin; detail from a map of 1375

with libraries and schools. The use of earth, straw, wood and mud plaster was designed to withstand the intense African sun, and many structures still stand today, such as the Djinguereber mosque in Timbuktu.

After Mansa Musa, the Kingdom of Mali was ruled by a succession of less successful monarchs who argued over who should rule the empire and squandered its riches. In 1433, Sonni Ali led a rebellion in Gao and founded the Songhai kingdom. By 1502 Mali was officially conquered

The Djinguereber Mosque in Timbuktu, commissioned by Mansa Musa in 1327

and for the next 150 years the Songhai continued to expand the territories under their control to monopolise on the taxation to be gained from the trans-Saharan trade routes.

Check your understanding

1. How did the Kingdom of Ghana gain wealth and power?
2. Which region of Africa did Sundiata rule?
3. How did the Mansas display their power?
4. Why did Mansa Musa become internationally recognised?
5. How did the Mansas of Mali display their power?

Kingdom of Benin

The Kingdom of Benin was one of the longest lasting states in West Africa, ruling from 1180 to 1897.

The Kingdom of Benin was ruled by the **Edo** people and existed in the forests of southern Nigeria. Its capital city was Edo (modern-day Benin City in Nigeria), but some people in the empire called it Ubini from which the word Benin originates.

Origins of the Oba

Traditional African beliefs are based on a world view called **animism**. This is centred on an understanding that objects, places and creatures can all possess spiritual qualities. Supernatural powers therefore animate the natural world on Earth. Humans must ensure a harmonious relationship with the environment through songs, dances, festivals and rituals, which have been passed down through centuries of oral history.

For the Edo people, the king was known as the **Oba** and held supernatural powers. Legend has it that the first Oba was crowned after the Edo **uzama** (village chiefs) sent a messenger to a sacred town of Ile Ife, requesting a divine ruler to restore order after a period of discord. The spirits sent Eweka, who was crowned around 1180.

The Oba was so sacred that there were special laws about who could speak to him or how closely they could approach him. He was shrouded in mystery and people would be punished for suggesting that he did human acts like sleeping, washing or eating. The Oba was rarely seen outside the palace, so ruled in parallel with the uzama. Nevertheless, all political and spiritual power was ultimately held by the Oba himself.

Oba Ewuare

In the early 15th century, power struggles erupted in the Kingdom of Benin, and Prince Ogun was exiled from the city by his brother. Legend has it that Ogun wandered through the African bush, performing rituals for the spirits. The spirits gave him a magic bag from which he could pull out whatever he desired. When he removed a thorn from a lion's paw, he was given a magical **talisman** that would grant any situation he wished for.

An Oba of the Benin Kingdom progressing on horseback outside Benin city, circa 1668

When sleeping under a tree one night, the spirits told Ogun he was ready to reclaim his throne. Ogun used the talisman to set fire to parts of Edo and his magic bag to pull out a poison arrow to assassinate his brother. In 1440 Ogun became the Oba of Benin and took the name **Ewuare**, meaning 'the trouble has ceased'.

The war with his brother had destroyed much of Edo, so Oba Ewuare rebuilt the city and expanded the Kingdom of Benin. He constructed a huge palace complex including shrines, meeting chambers, storehouses, craftsmen quarters and residential sections. Long galleries were held up by wooden pillars covered in copper, brass and bronze plaques known as the **Benin Bronzes**. Intricately carved ivory tusks were also positioned throughout the palace.

The city of Edo covered 6,500 square kilometres and was surrounded by earthwork trenches and high walls. The city was organised and divided into different sections according to its relationship to the Oba. For example, specialised crafts and ritual services were grouped in the same areas. This showed how the divine power of the mysterious Oba was embedded into all elements of life at Edo.

The Benin Bronzes

The Benin Bronzes are a collection of metal plaques and sculptures from the 16th century onwards that were looted from the palace at Edo by the British in 1897. In West African animist culture, blacksmiths are considered to wield magical powers, allowing them to transform metals into intricate objects. In Edo, blacksmiths lived in the Oba's palace and were employed to make items that narrated his lineage and exploits. As such, the bronzes are crucial evidence for learning about Benin's social and political history.

Benin bronze showing a warrior with two attendants and followers in the background

The power of women in West Africa

The traditional animist beliefs of West Africa emphasised the balance of male and female forces, and their politics reflected this. Women had authority to give orders, make decisions and enforce obedience. Women's councils met to discuss political matters in conjunction with men and took group action against those who mistreated members of the community. For example, female leaders could call on all women of the town to encircle a house, drag out an offending man and sit on him, ritually humiliating him in front of the community.

The Kingdom of Dahomey (what is now Benin) had all-female military units that were considered equal in strength and bravery to the men.

In the Kingdom of Benin, the **iyoba** (queen mother) was believed to have divine qualities and knowledge of traditional medicine. She was also a military commander, with her own regiment of soldiers. Bronze sculptures and ivory masks survive that commemorate Queen Idia, a famous 16th-century iyoba who led military campaigns to ensure her son Esigie became the Oba.

A brass sculpture of Queen Idia

Check your understanding

1. What did the uzama do in 1180?
2. According to legend, how did Oba Ewuare regain his kingdom?
3. In what ways did Oba Ewuare transform the city of Edo?
4. What do the Benin Bronzes show?
5. How did animist beliefs contribute to the way power was wielded in the Kingdom of Benin?

Great Zimbabwe

In the modern state of Zimbabwe, impressive stone ruins show the existence of a powerful medieval kingdom in southern Africa.

One of the first known kingdoms in southern Africa was **Mapungubwe**, in the Limpopo river valley. It emerged during the late 11th century. It had rich grazing lands for cattle, and the people made pottery and traded gold and ivory. There was a hierarchical society with leaders living on top of Mapungubwe Hill, separated from the other inhabitants below.

Elite burials show individuals with thousands of gold and glass beads. Impressive objects such as a wooden rhino, mace and headdress covered in thin sheets of gold have also been found. During the early 13th century, the Kingdom of Mapungubwe went into decline as better sources of gold were found.

The golden rhinoceros of Mapungubwe, made between 1220 and 1290

The ruins of Great Zimbabwe

From 1220, the Shona people organised a new southern African kingdom on the site of **Great Zimbabwe**. This was the largest commercial centre in southern Africa, controlling the trade in ivory, gold, iron and copper from the interior to the Swahili coast.

Great Zimbabwe's ruins cover 7.2 square kilometres and are the largest pre-colonial structures in sub-Saharan Africa. The walls reach up to 11 metres high, and over 1 million stones were used in their construction. Even more impressive is the lack of mortar holding the stones in place.

The site of Great Zimbabwe can be divided into three parts: the Hill, the Valley and the Outer City. The steep sides of the Hill dominate the landscape with walls built on the summit around the natural rock. It was here that archaeologists discovered monolithic soapstone pillars with carved birds on top. The Hill was probably where the leaders of the kingdom lived, overlooking the view across the Valley.

The Valley contains at least a dozen settlements with stone walls. The most distinctive element are the walls and solid conical tower known as the Great Enclosure. This large oval space is surrounded by almost 245 metres of stone walls that are over 5-metres thick in places. Narrow passageways run between an inner and outer wall, creating different routes, perhaps used by different social ranks so they didn't see each other. Some have argued that this was a religious compound, a residence for the king's wives or an initiation centre for young women.

Finally, the Outer City shows evidence of densely crowded houses, often made of **dhaka** (soil containing clay and gravel) with thatched roofs. Around 20 000 people may have lived in the city.

The Great Zimbabwe ruins

The Great Enclosure at the Great Zimbabwe Ruins

Colonial interpretations

In the 19th century, most European archaeologists who visited Great Zimbabwe refused to believe that a Black African civilisation could have made such impressive stone buildings. Even though Gertrude Caton-Thompson proved in 1929 the ruins were the work of the indigenous Shona people, efforts were made by the White colonial authorities to connect the ruins to cities in the Bible, as well as ancient Egyptians, Greeks or Phoenicians.

The Kingdom of Mutapa

From 1430, Great Zimbabwe was abandoned in favour of areas further north, perhaps due to a series of droughts. It is said that a prince from Great Zimbabwe founded the **Kingdom of Mutapa**, which conquered territories across modern Zimbabwe, Zambia, Mozambique and South Africa. The kingdom lasted until 1760.

Aspects of the Kingdom of Mutapa's social and political life were similar to those of Great Zimbabwe and Mapungubwe. For example, Mutapa religious beliefs were based on animism and worshipping royal ancestors. The Mutapa king was known as the **Mwene**, and he used oral historians to transmit stories of his deeds. The Mwene lived in a separate enclosure from the rest of his people and his symbols of power were a metal hoe, axe, and spear of gold and ivory. If states agreed to join the Mutapa empire without resistance, they were awarded with a seat on the Great Council. However, to ensure their loyalty, the Mwene kept the children of tribal chiefs as royal attendants at his capital in Zvongombe.

Check your understanding

1. What evidence shows a hierarchical society at Mapungubwe?
2. What types of ruins have been found at Great Zimbabwe?
3. How can we tell Great Zimbabwe was an important city?
4. What did Gertrude Caton-Thompson prove?
5. What can evidence from the Kingdom of Mutapa tell us about Mapungubwe and Great Zimbabwe?

Swahili city states

During the medieval period, the coastal **Swahili** city states of East Africa became vibrant global hubs for trade across the Indian Ocean.

The word Swahili comes from the Arabic 'sahil' meaning 'coast' and refers to the mixed African Bantu and Arabic language that emerged during this time. The Swahili coastal settlements stretched 1600 kilometres across the modern states of Kenya, Tanzania and Mozambique, and as far as the island of Madagascar. The largest port cities were Mombasa, Malindi, Zanzibar, Sofala and **Kilwa** whose sheltered harbours and coastal islands protected ships and kept waters calm.

Zanzibar **dhow** arriving from mainland Tanzania with goods such as fruits, vegetables, charcoal and timber

Merchants from the Islamic world, as well as India, Southeast Asia and sometimes China, sailed across the Indian Ocean to these ports. Here, they would buy products from the African interior, such as gold and ivory from Great Zimbabwe, and food such as bananas and yams. The people of the Swahili city states grew wealthy from their global trade. What is more, the integration of local African and Arab traditions created a distinctive Swahili culture.

Governing the Swahili city states

There were around 40 city states on the Swahili coast. Each was ruled independently by local leaders who had gained huge wealth and power from the Indian Ocean trade. These leaders were a Muslim merchant class of mixed Arab and African ancestry. Each city state had its own government, though the trade networks brought the cities close together and many of the merchants from different cities were related to each other. It appears that being Muslim became a part of Swahili identity, in contrast to those who followed traditional African animist beliefs and were often enslaved.

While the Swahili city states were individually powerful enough to remain independent, official power was in the hands of the Kilwa Sultanate. This was established in the 10th century when a Muslim man, Ali ibn al-Hassan Shirazi, sailed to the island of **Kilwa** off the coast of Tanzania and established himself as an Islamic sultan. Later documents, known as *The Kilwa Chronicle*, claim that his father was a Persian noble and his mother an enslaved African, legitimising his rule by giving him mixed African and Islamic ancestry.

Power was not centralised due to the wealth of the individual city states, but the sultan acted as a figurehead for the Islamic merchant class in East Africa. The wealth and power of the city states was generated from their merchants, trading the products arriving from Arabia, China, India and Southeast Asia with those coming from the African interior. They built sailing boats called dhows for

> ### Fact
>
> One of the most expensive products traded in the Swahili city states was **ambergris**. This odourless waxy substance from the intestines of sperm whales is expelled as vomit or excrement and found floating in tropical seas. It is important for making perfumes last longer on the skin.

Illustration of 1572 showing Kilwa, on the Tanzanian coast

ocean trade and long canoes for transporting goods along rivers from the interior to their coastal ports. Both were made from the timber, bark and leaves of the coconut palm tree.

The Shirazis ruled the Sultanate until 1277 when they were overthrown by Abu Moaheb. His family continued to rule the Kilwa Sultanate until the early 16th century. From that point onwards, the Swahili city states began to decline, as Portuguese merchants found their own routes to East Africa and rivalled the Swahili merchants' domination of Indian Ocean trade.

Architecture at Kilwa

Some of the most impressive medieval ruins from the Swahili city states survive at Kilwa. The Great Mosque is one of the oldest mosque structures in East Africa and has impressive octagonal columns, a multiple domed roof and 30 arches built of coral blocks, which were plastered and painted. Its wooden doors and window frames were intricately carved with decorative patterns.

Ancient mosque ruins at Kilwa Kisivani

A huge palace was constructed for the sultan in Kilwa during the 14th century. The palace roofs were domed like the mosque, and it is believed that it held 100 rooms, plus a courtyard with tiered seating and a swimming pool. Within the palace, archaeologists have found glazed pottery and stoneware imported from China. This architecture shows that by the 14th century, Kilwa was one of the most important and richest of the Swahili city states.

Cowrie currency

Cowrie shells come from small sea snails that are most abundant on the Indian Ocean islands of Sri Lanka, Borneo and the Maldives. Arab merchants traded cowrie shells on the Swahili coast, as well as on trans-Saharan trade routes. African kingdoms traded their gold for cowrie shells and used them at first for decorative purposes, but increasingly as a form of currency. In the West-African kingdom of Kanem-Bornu for example, the king's annual revenue was said to be worth 30 million cowrie shells.

Cowrie shells

Check your understanding

1. Where is the Swahili coast?
2. What products were exported from the interior of Africa?
3. What did Ali ibn al-Hassan Shirazi do?
4. Why did the Swahili city states have their own separate governments?
5. What architectural evidence from Kilwa shows its wealth?

Knowledge organiser

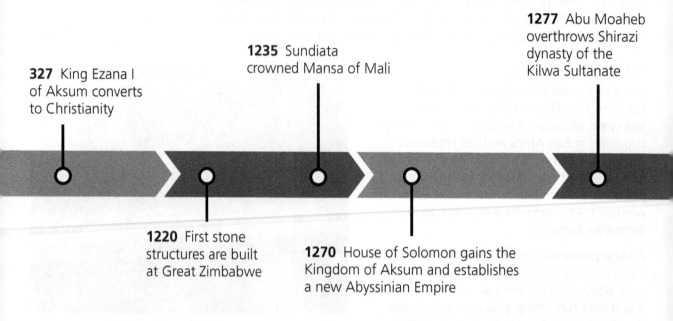

327 King Ezana I of Aksum converts to Christianity

1220 First stone structures are built at Great Zimbabwe

1235 Sundiata crowned Mansa of Mali

1270 House of Solomon gains the Kingdom of Aksum and establishes a new Abyssinian Empire

1277 Abu Moaheb overthrows Shirazi dynasty of the Kilwa Sultanate

Key vocabulary

Abyssinia Historical name for Ethiopia

Ambergris Expensive waxy substance from sperm whales that was traded on the Swahili coast

Animism Traditional African beliefs about spirits of the natural world

Ark of the Covenant Gold-covered wooden chest containing the two stone tablets with the Ten Commandments given to Moses

Benin Bronzes Collection of metal plaques from the 16th century onwards from the palace at Edo, looted by the British in 1897

Cowrie shells Shells from cowrie, a type of marine mollusc found in the Indian Ocean; the shells are used as currency in Africa

Dhaka Soil containing clay and gravel used to make houses at Great Zimbabwe

Dhows Types of trading ships in East Africa

Edo People who founded the Kingdom of Benin, and name of the capital city

Gbara Assembly in the Kingdom of Mali

Ge'ez Writing script of the Kingdom of Aksum

Great Zimbabwe Stone ruins found in modern Zimbabwe and centre of medieval kingdom

Gult Land grant given by the king in Abyssinia

House of Solomon Dynasty of the Ethiopian Empire founded in the 13th century, whose members claim descent from the Biblical King Solomon and the Queen of Sheba

Iyoba Name for queen mother in the Kingdom of Benin

Jeli Oral historian in the Kingdom of Mali

Kilwa Port city on the Swahili coast and base for the Kilwa Sultanate

Kingdom of Aksum Early medieval kingdom in modern Ethiopia

Kingdom of Benin Medieval kingdom in what is today southern Nigeria

Kingdom of Ghana Early medieval West African kingdom in modern Mauritania

Kingdom of Mali Kingdom that arose in the 13th century, controlling trans-Saharan trade

Kingdom of Mutapa Successor state to Great Zimbabwe in 15th century

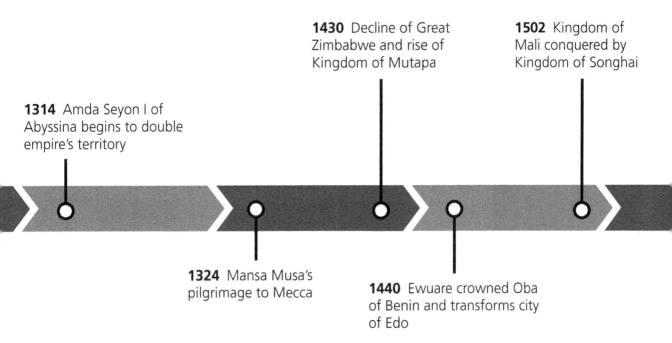

1430 Decline of Great Zimbabwe and rise of Kingdom of Mutapa

1502 Kingdom of Mali conquered by Kingdom of Songhai

1314 Amda Seyon I of Abyssina begins to double empire's territory

1324 Mansa Musa's pilgrimage to Mecca

1440 Ewuare crowned Oba of Benin and transforms city of Edo

Key vocabulary

Kurukan Fuga Charter of laws for the Mande people in Mali

Mansa Name for 'king' in the Kingdom of Mali

Mapungubwe Early medieval kingdom in southern Africa

Mwene Name for 'king' in the Kingdom of Mutapa

Oba Name for 'king' in the Kingdom of Benin

Obelisk Tall stone monument; in the ancient Kingdom of Axum they were used to mark a royal grave

Swahili Name for language of mixed African Bantu and Arabic

Talisman An object, such as a ring or stone, thought to have supernatural powers

Timbuktu Important city and centre of learning in the Kingdom of Mali

Uzama Village chiefs in the Kingdom of Benin

Key people

Ali ibn al-Hassan Shirazi First sultan of Kilwa in the 10th century

Frumentius Christian missionary who taught King Ezana I

Gertrude Caton-Thompson Archaeologist who proved that Great Zimbabwe was created by indigenous Shona people

King Ezana I King of Aksum who converted to Christianity

Mansa Musa Mansa of Mali who went on an internationally renowned hajj to Mecca

Menelik Supposed son of King Solomon, who is claimed to have transported the Ark of the Covenant to Abyssinia

Oba Eweka First Oba of Benin in 1180

Oba Ewuare Oba of Benin who transformed the city of Edo from 1440

Queen Idia Famous 16th-century iyoba of Benin

Sundiata First Mansa of Mali

The emperor and the people

One of the most powerful and most technologically advanced societies in the medieval world was the mighty empire of China.

Throughout the medieval period, the Chinese emperors ruled over a vast area of Asia containing a huge proportion of the world's people. By the 14th century there were perhaps 80 million people in China, in a world of fewer than 400 million. There were occasional civil wars and periods of disunity, but much of the time China remained united under a single emperor, and most of its people thought of themselves as members of a single civilisation – even though customs varied between regions.

Dynasties and emperors

The power of the emperor was believed to be divinely granted, and he was known as the 'Son of Heaven'. Beliefs about the nature of the emperor's divine status varied widely, but all agreed that he formed a link between humanity and Heaven. The emperor was seen as a semi-divine father to all Chinese people. Much of the emperor's role consisted of performing religious rituals that only he could conduct, fulfilling his place in the universal order that was thought to keep the world peaceful and safe.

It was believed that an emperor had the right to govern because he had been granted the **mandate of Heaven** – Heaven had given him its favour and supported his power. To keep the mandate, the emperor had to govern justly and rule in the interests of the whole country. The mandate was usually thought to stay with a single **dynasty** of emperors as long as they ruled in accordance with Heaven's will; so when the empire was troubled by famine, invasion or other disasters, this was often interpreted to mean that the mandate had been withdrawn and Heaven was no longer pleased with the ruling dynasty. If a rebel or invading group could successfully seize the throne, the mandate of Heaven had passed to them.

The three major dynasties of Imperial China were the **Tang dynasty** (618–907), the **Song dynasty** (960–1279) and the **Ming dynasty** (1368–1644).

- Under the three-century rule of the Tang, China became immensely prosperous and powerful. The collapse of the Tang in 907 was followed by the chaotic 'Five Dynasties and Ten Kingdoms Period', but order was re-established with the foundation of the Song dynasty in 960.

- The Song era saw industrial and technological progress that made China remarkable in the medieval world. Eventually, the Song were overwhelmed by Mongol conquerors who ruled China for almost a century.

The First Emperor

The power of the emperors started with Qin Shi Huang, who founded the first imperial dynasty in 221 BCE. His own dynasty lasted only until 207 BCE, but from that date onwards the imperial system endured.

Qin Shi Huang, the first emperor

- In 1368 a Chinese rebellion overthrew the Mongols and founded the Ming dynasty. The Ming restored Chinese traditions, and in many ways brought China back to the heights of power it had under the Tang.

Gentry and civil service

Below the emperor, powerful regional families, called the gentry, ran much of the local government in China's many provinces. Although the gentry held large amounts of land, the emperors could shift this land around at will, taking property from one gentry family and giving it to another, thus keeping the gentry from becoming too powerful.

Dragons are common in Chinese art, as on this gilt-carved bronze furnace from the Ming period

More powerful and more important than the gentry was China's complex **civil service**. The main duties of civil servants (**mandarins**) were taking the census, calculating and collecting taxation, and serving as judges. Civil servants had great power but were expected to live by an ideal of selfless loyalty and service to the emperor. To be part of the civil service, young men had to pass two or three stages of imperial examinations. These examinations focused on the arts of government and on the morality and traditions found in China's literature and philosophy. Most of those who were recruited through these examinations came from the gentry, but young men from poor backgrounds did sometimes pass. These examinations were extremely competitive, and some men spent their entire lives studying towards them.

In the imperial court, the emperor was attended by **eunuchs**. These men were trusted to serve the emperor selflessly because they could not have families of their own, so could not pass it on to their children – and therefore had less reason to gather power or wealth to themselves.

Pronouncing Chinese names

In the **Pinyin** transliteration system (the standard way of writing the Chinese language using the Western alphabet), these rules apply:

- 'q' is pronounced 'ch', as in *charm* or *chocolate*
- 'x' is pronounced roughly like the 'sh' in *shirt* or *shallow*
- 'zh' is pronounced 'j' as in *jam* or *jet*
- 'ou' is pronounced 'o' as in *go* or *hippo*.

Check your understanding

1. What did imperial Chinese people believe about the role of their emperor?
2. What was the mandate of Heaven?
3. What were the three major dynasties of Imperial China?
4. How did young men become members of the Chinese civil service?
5. What made Chinese emperors so powerful?

Unit 9: Imperial China
Family and society

Chinese society was strictly hierarchical. Everybody had their proper place, and all were expected to show obedience and submission to those above them.

Fathers, army commanders, civil service officials and all other men in positions of authority were expected to exercise firm discipline over those below them. It was expected that children would obey their fathers, wives would obey their husbands, and all Chinese people would obey the government or military officials who were their superiors. These values were based on a moral system called **Confucianism**.

Confucianism came from the teachings of the ancient Chinese philosopher Confucius, who lived in the 6th and 5th centuries BCE. Confucius taught that honour, duty and knowing your place were all-important. He said that people should be honest and careful, always obey their superiors, and work to improve themselves through learning. The classic Confucian texts (many of them written by Confucius's followers) were seen as the main source of moral guidance in China.

Village life

The majority of Chinese people were peasants who lived in small villages. They spent most of their lives working to grow crops, usually rice. Taxes were paid every year, often in grain and cloth, and the amount to be paid was the same no matter how rich or poor a family was, so the system was especially harsh on the poorest families. When times grew too hard, peasants sometimes joined secret societies of bandits or rebels, and peasant uprisings were quite common – but they were almost always suppressed by imperial troops.

Women in China had little independence. They were usually expected to stay at home and show total submission to men. All marriages were arranged, and women's options to own or inherit property were limited. In the Confucian worldview, men and women were seen as occupying separate roles, with women in an inferior position.

From the Song dynasty onwards, all Chinese households were grouped together in units of ten, and these tens into hundreds. Within each set of households, everybody was responsible for keeping watch on each other's behaviour and reporting anybody who acted in an improper or dishonourable way. This was called the **baojia** system.

Terraces for growing rice, in Guilin, north-east China, first built around 1270

Foot-binding

When they were small girls, Chinese women would often have their feet bound so tight that the bones in their feet or toes often broke. The binding prevented the feet from growing, so they would remain small enough to fit very small shoes. This was considered a mark of beauty and social status. Peasant women did not have this done – it would have prevented them working in the fields, because foot-binding could make it difficult to walk.

There were many attempts to end foot-binding, but the practice was not discontinued until the 20th century.

X-ray of a woman's bound feet

Religion in China

Unlike medieval Europe, China was a place where multiple religions co-existed, and the emperors usually showed respect for them all. It would have been unusual to suggest that only one religion could hold truth or value, as most people participated in rituals and traditions from differing faiths.

The most common organised religion was Buddhism. Buddhism was brought to China by missionaries from India in early medieval times, long before the rise of the Tang. Buddhist monks were just as respected as Confucian scholars, and Buddhist monasteries and temples covered the country. Monasteries were often major landowners and controlled huge estates. Because of their religious status, these monasteries were exempt from taxation and conscription, and so were all the monks and workers on their lands. This gave the monastic communities enormous social and financial power.

China's emperors were not always happy with the power of the Buddhist monasteries. Buddhism's focus on individual salvation, and its acceptance of everybody no matter what position they held in society, was deeply un-Confucian. Many people felt that Buddhism distracted people from their duties to their families and superiors. Emperor Wuzong, a Tang emperor who ruled in the 9th century, closed over 4000 monasteries in an attempt to seize their wealth and stop them from influencing the common people. However, incidents like this were rare. Generally, the monks respected the imperial system and promoted appropriate Chinese values of duty and submission to superiors. Some emperors were even Buddhists themselves.

The White Horse Temple in Luoyang – the oldest Buddhist temple in China, which dates from around 68 CE

The most widespread religion native to China was **Daoism**, which had few formal institutions and little hierarchical organisation. Daoists focused on attaining spiritual harmony with the Dao (often translated as the 'Way'), a spiritual force that connects and unites all things. All regions also had local nature gods, while the gentry and the emperors worshipped their own ancestors as protective spirits. In practice, Buddhism, Daoism and local cults mingled together to create a range of popular religious traditions.

Check your understanding

1. What were the main teachings of Confucianism?
2. What was believed to be the appropriate position of women in Chinese society?
3. What was the purpose of the baojia system?
4. Why were Chinese emperors sometimes suspicious of China's Buddhist monasteries?
5. What made the imperial Chinese religious landscape so different to medieval Christian Europe?

Trade and industry

Imperial China formed the centre of a trade network stretching across **Eurasia**, and saw the development of important new techniques in production and **commerce**.

Under the Tang dynasty, Chinese travellers and merchants ventured all over Asia, and created long-distance trade networks that connected China with many corners of the world. Much of this trade took place along the **Silk Road** – not an actual road, but a general set of routes through central Asia that connected China with India, Persia, the Arab world, the Byzantine Empire and ultimately Europe.

Booming trade

Regular contact with so many other regions made the cities of Tang China multi-ethnic and multicultural. **Chang'an**, the Tang capital (known today as Xi'an), was the biggest city on Earth in medieval times, with well over a million people. In the markets of Chang'an, merchants traded luxury goods including furs, spices, glassware and horses from the Ferghana Valley in central Asia. The city contained not only Buddhist temples but also Islamic mosques and even Christian churches, evidence of the empire's vast range of Eurasian connections. All this diversity reflected China's position at the centre of a network of connections across a huge number of places and cultures.

Internal trade within China also boomed. Much of this was made possible by the **Grand Canal**, an 1800-kilometre waterway linking China's two great rivers: the **Yellow River** (or Huang He) in the north and the **Yangzi River** in the south. Between 605 and 611 CE, over a million peasants are said to have laboured to create this canal, and unknown numbers died for it. The canal linked the agricultural regions of the south, which produced the bulk of China's food, with the major cities in the north. This meant that trade and food distribution across China became easier. Parts of the Grand Canal are still in use today, and it remains the longest artificial waterway in the world.

Modern ships carrying goods on the Grand Canal between Beijing and Hangzhou

Chinese pottery

Tang-era pottery, often considered the finest in the world, commonly featured figures of camels and traders on horseback – travellers on the Silk Road. Chinese pottery from this era onwards came to be widely considered the finest in the world.

Under the later Ming dynasty, pottery was made of **porcelain** – a strong and high-quality ceramic – and grew particularly popular in markets as far away as Europe.

Pottery figure of horse from the Tang dynasty (618–907)

Paper money

Booming commerce led to a very important invention: paper money. Previously, the Chinese had used circular coins with a square hole in the middle, that could be strung together on a string. As Chinese merchants grew richer, they found that storing and trading large quantities of coins in this way was inconvenient, and made them vulnerable to theft.

It was sensible to leave the coins somewhere safe, with a trusted person, and instead do business using **promissory notes**. These were slips of paper bearing a promise to swap them for coins when they were taken to the trusted person. Promissory notes could be carried and traded more easily than actual metal. Under the Song dynasty, emperors began issuing promissory notes themselves. These were the world's first true banknotes: paper money, issued by the government, that could be used for trade because everybody trusted that it could be swapped at any time for 'real' money.

Coins issued during the Song dynasty

Industry and the Song Dynasty

Under the Song, China experienced another remarkable period of economic growth. Much of the cause of this expansion was the discovery of a new rice variant called Champa rice, imported from a region in modern-day Vietnam. Champa rice grew fast enough that two harvests could be taken in a year. This massively increased the food supply and allowed farmers to sell more of their crop, so population and incomes both went up.

The result was a boom in **industry**, the processing of raw materials into manufactured goods. Iron and steel production became more widespread as the Chinese used coal-fired furnaces to produce massive quantities of metal goods, from weaponry to farm tools. In the year 1100, China was producing as much iron as all of Europe would be producing in the year 1700. At the same time, the arrival of the spinning wheel (probably invented in the Islamic world) made textile production much easier and cheaper. Before long, clothing, ceramics, printed books (see Chapter 5, this unit), and iron and steel tools were being mass-produced throughout China.

This period of commercial expansion lasted for around 200 years, during which time China was the most economically developed place in the world. Some historians believe that Song China can be seen as the only pre-modern example of a society experiencing sustained, ongoing industrial growth. It did not happen anywhere else in the world until the industrial revolution in 18th-century Britain.

Bronze bell from the Song Dynasty period.

Check your understanding

1. How was Imperial China connected by trade to much of the rest of the world?
2. What can we learn about Imperial China from the religious diversity of the city of Chang'an?
3. Why was the Grand Canal so important to the Chinese economy?
4. Why was paper money such an important invention?
5. Why did China become such an industrially active place under the Song dynasty?

Unit 9: Imperial China
Exploration and conquest

None of the other societies that China had contact with were as powerful or advanced. The emperors therefore thought of themselves as the natural rulers of the whole world.

The emperors saw China as the world's centre. They assumed that all other peoples in the world should submit to their superiority. Usually, this meant regular tribute and an acceptance of informal Chinese domination. However, sometimes it meant direct military invasion.

Up the Gansu Corridor

Throughout history, overland travellers heading west from China have had to travel up the **Gansu Corridor**: a narrow strip of hospitable land that runs between the Tibetan plateau to the south and the Gobi Desert to the north. It forms the gateway between the densely populated, fertile Chinese heartland and the open plains of central Eurasia. This made it a vital link in the Silk Road. China's emperors saw their control of the Gansu Corridor as vital, and frequently attempted to expand their power into the lands beyond.

The emperor who had the most success in central Asia was Taizong, the second emperor of the Tang dynasty and arguably China's greatest medieval conqueror. During the 630s and 640s, Taizong pushed the frontiers of Chinese rule up the Gansu Corridor and into Eurasia, overwhelming the Turkic peoples who controlled these lands at the time. Taizong's successors extended Chinese rule into what are now Kazakhstan and Afghanistan, and even parts of Persia. Control of these lands was never secure, and they were lost under later emperors.

Zheng He

The greatest explorer in Chinese history was the Muslim admiral Zheng He. Zheng lived in early Ming times under the Yongle emperor, a harsh ruler who is famous for building a grand imperial palace in Beijing called the **Forbidden City**. Beginning in 1405, the Yongle emperor commanded Zheng to lead a series of seven expeditions into the 'Western Ocean', to collect tribute from all corners of the world. Zheng eventually went on a total of seven voyages, the last one ending in 1433.

The largest of Zheng's ships were bigger than almost any wooden vessels in history, some being reported as being over 130 metres long. Zheng's fleet at its largest numbered almost 300 ships, with up to 27 000 men onboard.

Over the course of his seven voyages, Zheng visited Indonesia, India, Arabia and the Gulf, and many ports on the eastern coast of Africa. His fleet brought all the lands around the Indian Ocean into contact with China. However, the emperors who came after the Yongle emperor

> **Fact**
>
> The Chinese name for China – Zhongguo – translates as 'the **Middle Kingdom**' or, in modern times, 'the Central Country'.

Taiwanese stamp of 1962 showing Emperor Taizong (598–649), the second emperor of the Tang dynasty

were not interested in maintaining this contact. Instead, they forbade Chinese sailors from sailing anywhere except along the Chinese coastline. This was because most of the Ming emperors believed in a very strict and conservative interpretation of Confucianism, which taught that allowing merchants to make vast amounts of money would lead to corruption, while the arrival of new luxuries from foreign lands would disrupt the Chinese way of life. So, Zheng's voyages did not lead to official ongoing Chinese trade or conquest across the seas. Eventually, Zheng's ships rotted away, and the construction of replacements was forbidden.

Zheng He brought back many exotic gifts for the Chinese emperor – including some giraffes!

Empress Wu

Taizong's central Asian conquests would probably have been lost sooner if not for a remarkable ruler who came after him: the Empress Wu. Wu Zetian was brought into the imperial household by Taizong when she was only 13, to serve as a **concubine**. She later became an advisor to Taizong's much weaker-willed successor, Gaozong. Intelligent and ruthless, Wu gathered more power to herself as she betrayed or murdered her rivals in the court. When Gaozong suffered a stroke in 660, Wu became China's ruler in all but name. In 690 she formally took the throne herself as empress and ruled until her death in 705.

Statue of Empress Wu Zetian at Huangze Temple in Guangyuan, China

Wu was the only woman ever to officially sit on the Chinese imperial throne. She was a decisive commander who consolidated China's western empire, ensuring that it lasted for well over a century. She also conquered land in what is now Korea – something that Taizong had attempted and failed to do. The Empress Wu has been remembered as a vicious and immoral woman, but historians are still uncertain how much of her reputation is due to the writings of Chinese court historians who were angry that a woman had been their ruler.

Check your understanding

1. How did Chinese emperors view the world outside China?
2. Why was it considered so important for China to control the Gansu Corridor?
3. Why do some historians think that Empress Wu's poor reputation might not be deserved?
4. Why did Zheng He go on a series of voyages in the early 15th century?
5. Why did Zheng's voyages fail to establish continuing Chinese contact with the wider world via the seas?

Unit 9: Imperial China
Science and technology

Many inventions that would shape the history of the world were first developed in China, spreading to the rest of Eurasia from there.

Chinese tradition has long celebrated China's '**Four Great Inventions**', which are seen as Chinese civilisation's most significant technological contributions to the world. These are paper, printing, gunpowder, and the compass.

Paper and printing

Of these four inventions, paper was the oldest, first used long before medieval times. Traditionally, it was said to have been invented in the 2nd century CE by an imperial eunuch named Cai Lun. However, archaeologists have found paper fragments in China dating back to the 2nd century BCE. Paper was important because it made complex record-keeping easy and cheap, so it helped to make the imperial government powerful and efficient. It also enabled the invention of the world's first paper money.

Sometime in the early Tang period, the Chinese invented printing. Before printing, all books had to be copied by hand, which took a long time. In the 7th century, **woodblock printing** developed. This meant carving the characters of an entire page onto a large block of wood in reverse, then placing ink over the wooden block and pressing a sheet of paper onto it to create a print. This method still took a long time, but it meant that hundreds of copies could be made more easily.

In 868, the world's first surviving full printed book was made in China: a Buddhist text called the *Diamond Sutra*, complete with printed illustrations.

Woodblock printing

In the 1040s, under the Song, an artisan named Bi Sheng invented '**movable-type printing**'. Rather than carving a whole page, he carved individual characters that could then be re-arranged in any combination to create a page of writing. Bi Sheng's movable type was made of baked clay, though later movable-type printers in China used wood or bronze.

However, movable-type printing never became common in China for mass printing. Rather, woodblock printing remained dominant for centuries because Chinese writing uses thousands of different characters, so it was neither cheap nor convenient to create thousands of movable-type pieces. When the same technology was invented in Europe in the 15th century, it was adopted much more easily because the 26-letter Latin alphabet was better suited to it.

Chinese literature

Printing made it easier for Chinese literature to reach a wide audience. Under the Ming, some of the oldest and longest novels in the world were written, including three of China's 'Four Classic Novels' (the fourth came in the 18th century).

Gunpowder and the compass

The Song dynasty also saw the inventions of gunpowder and the compass. Gunpowder is an explosive chemical mixture of several naturally occurring substances, including sulphur and saltpetre. Under the Song, the Chinese used gunpowder to make fireworks. These were used to send signals for military purposes, or for display and celebration.

Song engineers also invented a primitive kind of gun, known as a 'fire lance'. However, Chinese armies only began using guns in warfare in late Ming times – around the same time as armies in Europe, where the technology had spread via the Ottoman Turks. Under the Ming, simple muskets were used alongside the traditional crossbows in battle. Some generals began to use cannons in the defence of the Great Wall.

Cannon used by Chinese troops during the Ming dynasty

In the 11th century, Chinese explorers discovered that a naturally occurring magnetic ore called a **lodestone** would align itself in a north–south direction when suspended in water. We now know that this happens because of its attraction to the Earth's magnetic field. An iron or steel needle that was touched to the lodestone would become magnetic itself and always point north. This needle could then be used as a compass, making navigation vastly easier.

The Great Wall of China

Often claimed to be over 2000 years old, most of the **Great Wall of China** is actually a series of Ming fortifications built in the 16th and early 17th centuries. It was built to establish imperial power in the far north of the country, and to defend against attack by nomadic northern peoples such as the Mongols. The Great Wall was really a complex network of walls, towers, armouries, granaries, and military bases, instead of a single, continuous wall.

A section of the Great Wall of China

Check your understanding

1. Why was paper so important in Chinese society?
2. How does woodblock printing work?
3. Why did movable-type printing never become common in China?
4. How was the compass invented in Imperial China?
5. What purposes was gunpowder used for in Imperial China?

Knowledge organiser

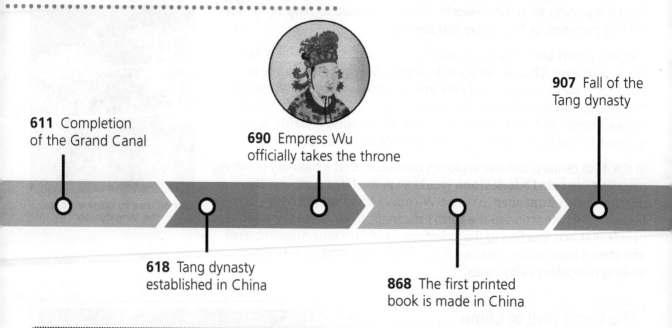

611 Completion of the Grand Canal

690 Empress Wu officially takes the throne

907 Fall of the Tang dynasty

618 Tang dynasty established in China

868 The first printed book is made in China

Key vocabulary

Baojia System of social organisation under which all households in China were grouped in units to keep watch on and support each other

Chang'an Capital city of China under the Tang dynasty, today known as Xi'an

Civil service The permanent staff of a government, responsible for administering the country

Commerce The activity of buying and selling, usually by merchants

Concubine A woman who lives with a married man but is not married to him, and is considered to have lower status than the man's wife

Confucianism Moral philosophy based on the teachings of the ancient philosopher Confucius, focused on duty, honour and self-improvement

Daoism Chinese religion focused on being in harmony with the Dao, a spiritual force believed to connect and unite the whole universe

Dynasty A family that holds power, usually as rulers, with power being passed from parent to child over generations

Eurasia Europe and Asia combined, which makes up the largest continental landmass in the world

Eunuch A man who has been castrated and therefore cannot have children

Forbidden City Large palace complex in Beijing, built to serve as the main residence of Chinese emperors and centre of Chinese government

Four Great Inventions Traditional list of Chinese inventions considered the most significant: paper, printing, gunpowder and the compass

Gansu Corridor Also known as the Hexi Corridor, a narrow strip of land between the Tibetan plateau and the Gobi Desert, forming a 'gateway' that connects the coastal Chinese heartland with central Asia

Grand Canal Artificial waterway linking the Yellow River with the Yangzi River, essential for Chinese food distribution and commerce

Great Wall of China System of fortifications in China's far north, built to defend against nomadic northern peoples

Industry The processing of raw materials into manufactured or consumable goods

Lodestone Naturally occurring magnetised stone

Mandarin European term for a Chinese civil servant

Mandate of Heaven Permission to rule over China, believed to be granted by the gods to a dynasty or to a specific emperor

Enquiry Question: Was Imperial China a place where nothing ever really changed, or a place of new beginnings?

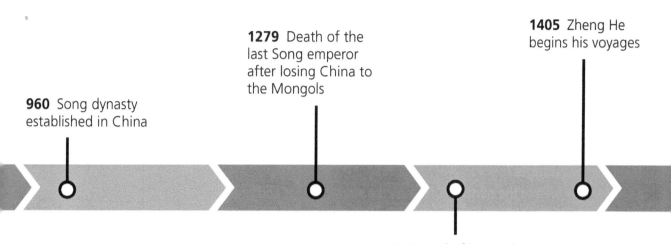

1279 Death of the last Song emperor after losing China to the Mongols

1405 Zheng He begins his voyages

960 Song dynasty established in China

1368 End of Mongol rule and foundation of the Ming dynasty

Key vocabulary

Middle Kingdom Chinese name for China, often translated as 'Central Country' in modern times

Ming dynasty Imperial dynasty that ruled China from 1368 to 1644, restoring Chinese independence after a period of Mongol rule

Movable-type printing A system of printing that uses and rearranges individual letters or characters and punctuation

Pinyin The standard system for writing the Chinese language using the Latin (Western) alphabet rather than Chinese characters

Porcelain Strong and high-quality pottery, commonly made in China and often highly decorated

Promissory notes Slips of paper that bear a promise they can be swapped for coins or precious metal when taken to a trusted person

Song dynasty Imperial dynasty that ruled China from 960 to 1279, a period of technological innovation and industrial growth

Tang dynasty Imperial dynasty that ruled China from 618 to 907, a period of great power and prosperity

Woodblock printing Printing technique that uses a carved wooden block to print an entire page

Yangzi River Major river in the south of China

Yellow River Major river in the north of China, also called Huang He

Key people

Confucius Ancient Chinese philosopher whose teachings formed the basis of Chinese values in medieval times

Qin Shi Huang The first Chinese emperor, who founded the Chinese imperial government in 221 BCE

Taizong Tang emperor who conquered vast territories for China in central Asia

Wu Zetian Empress Wu, Tang ruler who was the only female emperor in Chinese history

Yongle emperor The third Ming emperor, who built the Forbidden City and sent Zheng He on his voyages

Zheng He Ming-era admiral who led seven great voyages of exploration around the Pacific and Indian oceans

Unit 10: The Mongols
Chinggis Khan

In the 13th century, a people called the Mongols carried out the most rapid and far-reaching series of conquests the world has ever known.

The Mongols conquered China, Russia, central Asia, and parts of India, the Middle East and Europe. Their first leader was Chinggis Khan, arguably the greatest warlord in the history of the world.

Who was Chinggis?

The Mongols lived to the north of China on the **steppe**, a flat and grassy region that stretches across much of Eurasia. Their **nomadic** lifestyle was based on horses. They learned to ride and shoot arrows from the age of three, lived in tents, ate meat but few vegetables, and drank mare's milk. Mongol women had much greater independence than most women in neighbouring China, and could hunt and fight alongside men. When Chinggis was born, around 1160, the Mongols were divided into many warring tribes.

Chinggis was originally named Temüjin, meaning blacksmith. His father was killed by a rival tribe when Temüjin was eight or nine, and he was left to fend for himself on the steppe. Soon he became a follower of Toghril, the most powerful **khan** (chieftan) in Mongolia. But Temüjin's intelligence and strong personality won him followers of his own, and eventually he defeated Toghril in battle and went on to unite the Mongol tribes under his leadership. The Mongols believed in giving loyalty to rulers who were successful in war, so Temüjin's military skill won him widespread support. By 1206 he was **khagan** (supreme ruler) of all the Mongols. Temüjin was given the title Chinggis Khan, meaning 'Fierce Lord'.

Chinggis Khan

Chinggis valued loyalty above all else, but he was ruthless to his enemies. After becoming khagan, Chinggis began a series of conquests that would last for the rest of his life. These conquests were at first driven by many factors, including Chinggis' need to keep his men's loyalty by success in war and his desire to win control of the trade routes along the **Silk Road**. However, the conquests soon went beyond these original motives, growing into a seemingly endless expansion of Mongol power.

Chinggis at war

The first place that Chinggis attacked beyond the steppe was the Jin empire that ruled northern China. Chinggis invaded in 1211 and had conquered most of their territories by 1215. Next, he turned towards the west. Most of central Asia at this time was ruled by an Islamic state called the **Khwarazmian Empire**. Originally, Chinggis seems to have had no intention of attacking them; instead, he sent a caravan of Mongol **envoys** to a Khwarazmian border town named Otrar, to request peace and the right to trade. However, the governor of Otrar massacred these Mongol envoys. Chinggis then sent an envoy directly to the Khwarazmian **Shah** (ruler), demanding that the governor be handed over to the Mongols for punishment. The Shah had the envoy killed.

Determined to punish them, Chinggis invaded the Khwarazmian Empire in 1219. Two of central Asia's greatest cities, **Bukhara** and **Samarkand**, were dramatically **sacked** in order to set an example of what the Mongol horde could do. After capturing Bukhara, Chinggis is said to have gathered the leading men of the city in their mosque and declared before them: "I am the scourge of God."

Neighbouring cities submitted immediately rather than risk the same fate, and the Khwarazmian Shah fled to an island in the Caspian Sea. Meanwhile, the Shah's son fled south into Persia, where Chinggis pursued him and conquered yet more cities. Chinggis then split his forces in two. He led an army east through Afghanistan into northern India before heading back northward into Mongolia. Meanwhile, his generals Sübetei and Jebe led their hordes westward through Persia, then turned north to move through the **Caucasus** – the mountainous land bridge that connects the Middle East with southern Russia. After vanquishing a Russian army, Sübetei and Jebe returned to Mongolia to reunite with Chinggis.

All this success was due to the Mongols' tough, disciplined cavalry army, with men trained in hunting and fighting from early childhood. Chinggis also understood the power of fear: often he would dramatically sack one city in order to terrify a whole region into surrendering. When Chinggis Khan died in 1227, he had conquered more of the world than anybody in human history.

Fact

The Mongols learnt new tactics quickly. Despite having no experience of siege warfare, Chinggis was quick to realise how powerful siege weapons could be. He took the city of Nishapur in Persia in 1221 by using 3000 giant crossbows and 300 catapults.

A modern re-enactment of a Mongol horde

Check your understanding

1. What made the culture of the Mongols unusual?
2. How did Chinggis Khan become khagan of all the Mongols?
3. Why did Chinggis attack the Khwarazmian Empire?
4. What regions of the world had the Mongols conquered by the time of Chinggis' death in 1227?
5. What was the purpose of sacking cities such as Bukhara and Samarkand?

Unit 10: The Mongols
The Mongol conquests

The expansion of Mongol power did not end with the death of Chinggis. His sons and followers went on to conquer even more of the world.

Chinggis' chosen successor as khagan of the Mongols was his third son, Ögedei. After taking the throne, Ögedei completed the conquest of the Jin empire, which surrendered in 1234. Then, in 1236, he sent two armies westward: one to Persia and one to Russia.

The army heading into Persia, led by a general named Chormaqan, successfully completed its conquest. The army that headed into Russia was commanded by Chinggis' grandson Batu and the veteran general Sübetei. In Russia, they applied the Mongol tactic of massacring a few entire cities in order to terrify the rest of the population into submission. In the city of Vladimir, when the prince, bishop, nobles and all their families took refuge in a church, the Mongols locked the church doors and burned it to the ground.

In 1240, Batu and Sübetei took the greatest Russian city, **Kyiv**, and settled their horde on the lower Volga River. This was the beginning of a new Mongol empire in Russia, that would soon be called the **Golden Horde**.

After subduing Russia, Batu and Sübetei headed even further west into Europe. They defeated armies of Poles, Hungarians and the famous order of **Teutonic Knights**, who were said to be among the greatest warriors in Europe. After one battle, the Mongols paraded a display of nine sacks, all filled with severed ears of the dead. Terrified Europeans tried to find Biblical explanations for the Mongol attacks – some people identified them with Gog and Magog, mentioned in the Book of Revelation as monsters who will come at the end of time.

Hungarian woodcut of 1488 showing Mongols carrying off captives from Galicia and Volhynia (modern-day Poland and Lithuania)

Möngke

In 1241, having reached as far west as Austria, Batu and Sübetei heard of the death of Ögedei, and withdrew from Europe. Mongol khans from across Eurasia headed back to the steppe and gathered in the new city of **Karakorum**, which Ögedei had founded as a Mongol capital.

Now the Mongols had to choose a new khagan. Unfortunately, there was no qualification to be leader

Karakorum today

of the Mongols except being descended from Chinggis. The assembly did not choose their new khagan, Ögedei's son Güyük, until 1246. Even then, fighting and plotting continued for years. Eventually, another of Chinggis' grandsons, Möngke, seized power in 1251, and succeeded in winning the loyalty of most of the khans.

Under Möngke, the Mongols once again invaded the Arab world. On New Year's Day 1256, Möngke's younger brother Hülegü led a great horde across the Amu Darya River in central Asia, aiming to conquer the Middle East. In 1258 they captured Baghdad, and the last Abbasid caliph was murdered. Because they believed they might be cursed if they shed his blood, the Mongols killed the caliph by rolling him up in a carpet and then trampling him to death with their horses.

The horde had conquered Syria and was about to invade Egypt when news came of Möngke's death. Hülegü led much of his army back into central Asia. Those who remained were defeated on 3 September 1260 at a place called **Ayn Jalut**, or Goliath's Spring. The people who beat them were the Mamluks, local Muslim rulers who themselves had originally come from central Asia. **Ayn Jalut** was the first major defeat that a Mongol army had ever suffered in battle. It is often seen as marking the end of the era of Mongol expansion.

Divided hordes

In theory, the khagan of the vast Mongol empire was now Kublai Khan, another grandson of Chinggis. However, in 1260–4 there was yet another period of warfare over the succession. At its end, the Mongol conquests were divided into four, with different territories becoming separate khanates under independent khans:

- Kublai kept Mongolia and China, a territory now known as the Khanate of the Great Khan.

- The Golden Horde held on to power in Russia and eastern Europe.

- Central Asia came to be ruled by the Chaghatayid Khanate, named after Chinggis' second son Chaghatay.

- Hülegü became ruler of the Il-Khanate ('lesser khanate') of Persia, which contained not only Persia but also Mesopotamia (modern Iraq) and parts of Asia Minor.

> **Fact**
>
> Chinggis Khan only fathered six children that we know of, but modern geneticists have suggested that one in 200 men alive today are his direct descendants.

Reconstruction of a traditional Mongolian dwelling-yurt at Sarai Batu, the capital of the Golden Horde

---

Check your understanding

1. What new empire did Batu and Sübetei establish by their conquests in the 1230s?

2. Why did Batu and Sübetei withdraw from Europe in 1241?

3. Why did it take so long for the Mongols to choose a new khagan after Ögedei's death?

4. Why is the defeat at Ayn Jalut remembered as a significant moment in Mongol history?

5. Why had the Mongol empire not remained united by the later 13th century?

Unit 10: The Mongols
Kublai Khan and China

One of the greatest Mongol rulers was Kublai Khan, who was both the Mongol khagan and the Emperor of China.

Conquering China

At the time of the first Mongol conquests under Chinggis, the Song dynasty that had ruled China for centuries was already weak. The emperors had lost huge amounts of land to a people called the **Jurchen**. These were a semi-nomadic people with a culture similar to the Mongols, who came from the eastern steppe region of Manchuria. In the 1120s, almost a century before Chinggis, the Jurchen had taken over all of northern China and founded the Jin empire, while the Song kept control only south of the Yangzi River. This meant that China was already divided between two powers long before the Mongols arrived.

When the Mongols began their expansion in the early 13th century, the Jin empire was easily conquered. Later, in 1258, the Mongols began launching attacks on the remaining Song territories. To launch a full assault on the lands south of the Yangzi River, the Mongols first needed to capture the twin cities of Xiangyang and Fancheng. These two heavily fortified cities stood on either side of the Han tributary of the Yangzi River and controlled access to the south.

Kublai Khan besieged the cities in 1267, beginning the six-year **Battle of Xiangyang**. Finding that his cavalry was all but useless against fortifications and warships on the river, Kublai called for reinforcements from across his empire: sailors from Korea, Muslim siege engineers from central Asia, and Chinese troops from the north. Even so, the siege was only broken when Kublai's siege engineers built several mighty **trebuchets**, each capable of hurling rocks weighing up to 100 kg. The cities fell in 1273, and Kublai's forces pushed southward. When the last Song emperor committed suicide in 1279, all of China was under Kublai's rule.

Modern statue of Kublai Khan at the Site of Xanadu in Mongolia, China, the summer capital city of the Yuan dynasty

The Yuan dynasty

Kublai was fascinated by Chinese culture and eager to adopt the traditions, as well as the power, that came with being a Chinese emperor. In 1272 he announced that he was founding a new Chinese imperial family, the **Yuan dynasty** (although historians usually date its rule from 1279, the end of the Song). Kublai ruled through established Chinese structures of government and fulfilled the ritual role of a Chinese emperor. Some other Mongols found his acceptance of a Chinese lifestyle ridiculous; they felt that living in the manner of a **sedentary** people (those who were not nomadic) was beneath the dignity of a Mongol khan.

It is often said that China changed the Mongols more than the Mongols changed China. This means that Kublai and his followers lived and ruled in Chinese ways without forcing Chinese people to adopt Mongol ways. However, Kublai did put laws in place to keep native Chinese people subservient. The Chinese were forbidden to learn the Mongol language, wear Mongol dress or marry Mongols; they were also forbidden from carrying weapons. Foreigners were also brought in to run the civil service in place of native Chinese.

Kublai died in 1294 after years of ignoring his kingdom in favour of feasting and luxuries. By the time of his death, he was obese and was drunk most days. His successors ruled China for another 70 years, but few of them were good emperors. They were finally overthrown by a peasant rebel movement called the **Red Turbans**, who allied with Chinese gentry and officials to form a united front against the Mongols.

Beijing

Kublai wished to move his capital into the heart of China, abandoning Karakorum on the steppe. He chose to build a new city on the site of what had been Zhongdu, the capital of the Jin empire. The new city was built on a grand scale, with high walls enclosing a grid-based street plan. This became **Beijing**, and most Chinese rulers since Kublai have continued to use it as the country's capital.

Kamikaze

The most famous military failure of Kublai's reign was his attempt to conquer Japan. He sent two invasion fleets, in 1274 and 1281, but both the Mongol fleets were destroyed in massive typhoons. The Japanese believed that these storms had been sent by the gods to save them from conquest. They called them the *kamikaze*, meaning 'divine wind'.

Illustration of the Mongol invasion of Japan from *Dai Nihonshi* ('Great History of Japan'), completed between 1672 and 1906

In 1368 the Red Turbans forced the last Mongol armies out of China. Their leader, a Buddhist monk named Zhu Yuanzhang, took the title of the Hongwu emperor, which means the 'vastly martial' emperor. The Hongwu emperor's new dynasty was called the Ming. The Ming emperors restored Chinese independence, but they were distrustful of foreigners and strict about sticking to Chinese tradition. They were determined never to let China be overrun by foreigners again.

Check your understanding

1. Why was China already divided and weakened before the Mongol conquests?
2. Why did some Mongols feel that Kublai was wrong to adopt a Chinese lifestyle as emperor?
3. Why did Kublai fail to conquer Japan?
4. How did Mongol rule in China come to an end?
5. How were Chinese people oppressed by the Mongols during the rule of the Yuan dynasty?

Unit 10: The Mongols
The world of the Mongols

Although the Mongols conquered with great ferocity, they usually proved to be capable and just rulers. Their rule established new connections across much of Eurasia.

There was no standard form of Mongol government, but most preferred to rule with a light touch. When conquering new lands, they often simply took over the existing forms of government, leaving things mostly unchanged. There was a law code called the **Yasa**, a mixture of old steppe traditions and decrees by Chinggis, but it applied primarily to Mongols and other nomadic peoples, not to the sedentary peoples they ruled over.

Trade and the Silk Road

Since ancient times, goods from all over Eurasia had been traded along the Silk Road, the route through central Asia that linked China, Persia, India, the Middle East, the Byzantine Empire and Europe. Central Asia is sometimes called the crossroads of the medieval world because it connected so many different cultures. The great oasis cities of central Asia, such as Bukhara, Samarkand, Tashkent and Merv, formed the key stops on the Silk Road and were famously rich and beautiful. Their local rulers were often **Turkic**, one of the many different peoples who inhabited the region.

Registan square in the city of Samarkand, Uzbekistan, one of the most important sites on the Silk Road

Under the Mongols, travel and trade along the Silk Road became easier than ever before, as their rule brought stability and peace. This continued even when the various khanates were no longer united, as travel and communication between them remained smooth.

The Mongols established a network of postal stations along the roads of Eurasia, allowing messages to travel with great speed. The stations were spaced between 30 km and 60 km apart, so a messenger on horseback would arrive at a station exhausted after riding hard. He would then immediately give his message to a different messenger and stay to rest, while the new messenger rode on. This system was called the **Yam**.

When the Mongols did sack a city, they often deliberately spared the skilled craftsmen. These people were then brought to live on the steppe in small new towns dedicated to their crafts.

Fact

Though Chinggis Khan was illiterate, he created a written form of the Mongol language for the first time with the help of a captive, using a Turkic alphabet.

Mongol women

Mongol women had significantly more independence than women in many societies at the time. They could own and inherit their own property, and often held important religious positions. Some were warriors, including the famous Khutulun – a cousin of Kublai Khan, who was renowned as one of the great fighters of her time.

Mongolian woman in traditional dress

Religion and the Mongols

Most Mongol rulers had a tolerant attitude to religion. Chinggis Khan himself followed the Mongols' traditional religion, focused on the worship of the sky god Tängri. He seems to have believed that he was divinely guided and inspired by this god. He was also a deeply superstitious man who believed that it was safest to respect all known gods, so he kept company with priests and sages from every religion that the Mongols knew.

Under Chinggis' successors, this open attitude towards all religions became the most common official policy. Buddhists, Muslims, Christians and pagans of all kinds were able to live and worship freely within most of the lands ruled by the Mongols. Möngke even held a great debate between representatives of Christianity, Buddhism and Islam, with a Flemish monk named William of Rubruck arguing for Christianity (the debate did not end in any agreement).

In 1295, a Mongol ruler named Ghazan, who was the Il-Khan of Persia, converted to Islam. This was the first time that any khan had given up the Mongols' traditional religion. It showed that old steppe ways were being abandoned, as the Mongols adopted the lifestyles of the lands they had conquered.

Marco Polo

Marco Polo was the son of a Venetian jewel merchant who became a famous traveller in the khanates. Aged just 17, Marco set off with his father and uncle in 1271 on a mission to meet Kublai Khan. They were given a blessing from the Pope to convert Kublai to Christianity.

Some 25 years later, Marco Polo and his father returned to Venice. In 1298 Marco Polo published an account of his travels entitled *Description of the World*. The book told the extraordinary story of Marco Polo's journey to Beijing, his work as a military advisor to Kublai Khan, and his return to Europe escorting a Mongol princess to Persia.

Ever since its publication, people have wondered how much truth there is to Marco Polo's adventures. Some parts are clearly made up, such as his account of Prester John, a mythical Christian king who never actually existed. As for the time he spent in China, Polo accurately records their use of paper money and coal for fuel but neglects to mention anything about chopsticks or Chinese characters for writing. In contemporary sources from all the locations in China that Marco Polo claims to have visited, there is no single mention of a European advisor to Kublai Khan.

Statue of Marco Polo at Kublai Square in Zhenglan Banner, Mongolia

Check your understanding

1. What laws applied to people living under Mongol rule?
2. What was the Yam?
3. What was the usual Mongol policy towards different religions?
4. What story did Marco Polo's book *Description of the World* tell?
5. How did Mongol rule encourage travel and trade across Eurasia?

Timur

Just when the Mongol age seemed to be over, a terrifying new conqueror appeared who would gain a reputation as an even more brutal Mongol warlord than Chinggis.

This was **Timur Lenk**, or Timur the Lame – soon known in Europe as Tamerlane. Timur's ambition was to reunite the original Mongol empire through conquest. He would very nearly succeed in this aim.

Timur's conquests

Timur was born in a small town south of Samarkand in 1336, the son of a minor local chieftan. By this time, the Chaghatayid Khanate had broken up, and central Asia was once again divided between many smaller domains. Persia, to the south, was also no longer ruled by Mongols, as the Il-Khanate had collapsed in 1335 after decades of warfare with the Golden Horde.

Wall painting of Timur the Great at Tamerlane Museum, Uzbekistan

Timur claimed descent from Chinggis Khan, although his ancestry was probably mostly Turkic rather than Mongol. As a young man, he suffered a wound in battle that left him permanently paralysed down his right side and with a limp; this is why he became known as Timur the Lame. Timur was determined to win power and longed to restore the greatness of the lost Mongol empire built by Chinggis Khan.

Through a series of clever alliances and wars with local rulers, Timur eventually became ruler of Samarkand in 1369. A decade later, around 1380, he launched a series of extraordinary wars of conquest, leading his armies to attack not only other central Asian states but Persia, Afghanistan, Asia Minor, Russia and India. Although he did not conquer all these lands, he did carve out a massive empire that covered most of central Asia, all of Persia and Afghanistan, and parts of the lands around.

Timur's army contained troops drawn from everywhere he ruled, including, eventually, elephant cavalry from India. He became notorious for his cruelty as a warlord. In 1387, when he sacked the Persian city of Isfahan, all Timur's soldiers were ordered to bring a set number of heads to their commanders on pain of death. Immediately, a market in severed heads sprang up in the wrecked city. The price of a head fell from 20 dinars (the local currency) to half a dinar, as people rushed to behead each other just to meet the quotas. When Timur's court historian walked round the city afterwards, he counted 28 towers, each one built from 1500 severed heads.

> **Fact**
>
> At Timur's court in Samarkand there was a tree made of gold, with a trunk as thick as a man's leg and bearing fruit made of gemstones.

Timur was on his way to invade China when he died in 1405. Although he had created an empire, his achievements did not last. His descendants continued to rule parts of central Asia for a century as the Timurid dynasty, but most of his wider conquests were quickly lost.

By Timur's death, the Mongol empires were mostly a thing of the past. The Red Turbans had ended Mongol rule in China in 1368. The collapse of Timur's empire meant the end of Mongol rule in most of central Asia or Persia. The Golden Horde still ruled much of Russia, but by the mid-15th century their power was also failing (see box) and they were no longer a threat to Europe. The Mongols stayed in power only on the steppe, ruling their original homeland in much the same way as they had always done. However, their legacy was a far more interconnected Eurasian landmass than any time before in its history.

Timur's mausoleum in Samarkand, where he was buried

Russia and the Tatars

The Mongols of the Golden Horde who settled in Russia became known as **Tatars**, a name originally given to the first Mongol invaders of Europe. They ruled Russia for over two centuries, beginning with Batu and Sübetei's conquests in the 1230s. During this period, the southern parts of Russia remained under close Tatar control, but the cities further north – such as Moscow and Novgorod – had slightly more independence. They paid taxes and tribute to the Tatars, but the princes of these cities were slowly growing more powerful.

In 1462, a prince called Ivan III came to the throne in Moscow. He wanted to unite the Russian cities and throw off the control of the Golden Horde. In a series of conquests, Ivan brought all the major Russian cities under his rule. A massive Tatar attack on Moscow in 1481 was defeated, and Tatar rule ended. From this time onwards, the Tatars would have little power in Russia – though Tatar groups continued to live in and around Russia well into modern times.

The Ivan the Great Bell Tower in Moscow was built to honour him after his death

Ivan III became known as **Ivan the Great**. In many ways, by defeating the Tatars he created Russia as a unified nation for the first time. Ivan was also the first Russian ruler to call himself Tsar (a Russian version of the Roman name 'Caesar'). Russia's rulers from his time onwards continued to take this title.

Check your understanding

1. What was Timur Lenk's great ambition?
2. What parts of the world did Timur end up ruling?
3. How much of Timur's empire stayed united after his death in 1405?
4. How did resistance to the Tatars lead to the creation of a united Russia in the 15th century?
5. Why is Timur often remembered as a conqueror to rival Chinggis Khan?

Knowledge organiser

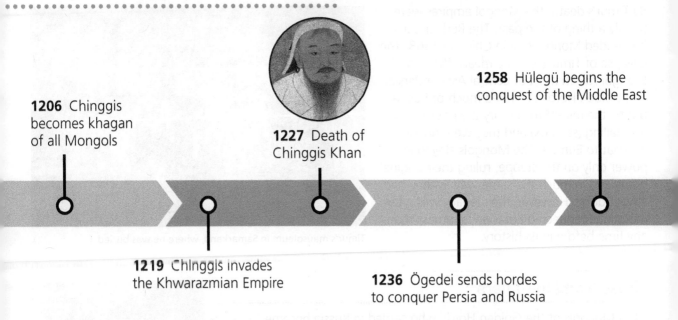

1206 Chinggis becomes khagan of all Mongols

1227 Death of Chinggis Khan

1258 Hülegü begins the conquest of the Middle East

1219 Chinggis invades the Khwarazmian Empire

1236 Ögedei sends hordes to conquer Persia and Russia

Key vocabulary

Ayn Jalut Meaning Goliath's Spring, site of the first major defeat suffered by a Mongol army

Battle of Xiangyang Six-year siege of Xiangyang and Fancheng that enabled Kublai to go on to conquer the south of China

Beijing City founded by Kublai Khan that has been the capital of China in most periods of Chinese history ever since

Bukhara Major Silk Road city in central Asia, now in Uzbekistan

Caucasus Mountainous land bridge that connects the Middle East with southern Russia

Envoy A messenger or representative, especially one on a diplomatic mission

Golden Horde Mongol empire that ruled large areas of Russia

Jurchen Steppe people with a culture similar to the Mongols, who conquered northern China about a century before Chinggis

Karakorum Mongol capital city on the steppe, founded by Ögedei

Khagan Mongol term for a supreme ruler who commands many khans

Khan Mongol term for a lord or chieftan

Khwarazmian Empire Islamic empire that ruled much of central Asia before Chinggis's conquests

Kyiv The greatest Russian city at the time of the Mongol conquests, now the capital of Ukraine

Nomadic Living a wandering life with no permanent home

Red Turbans Chinese rebel movement that overthrew their Mongol rulers, leading to the establishment of the Ming dynasty

Sack Plunder and destroy a city

Samarkand Major Silk Road city in central Asia, now in Uzbekistan

Sedentary Literally 'sitting', also used as the opposite of nomadic (to refer to people who live in permanent homes)

Shah Persian term for a king or emperor, used by the rulers of the Khwarazmian Empire among others

Silk Road An ancient overground trade route that linked East Asia with the West

Steppe Flat, vast plains that stretch across central Eurasia, covering large areas of eastern Europe, central Asia, southern Russia and Mongolia

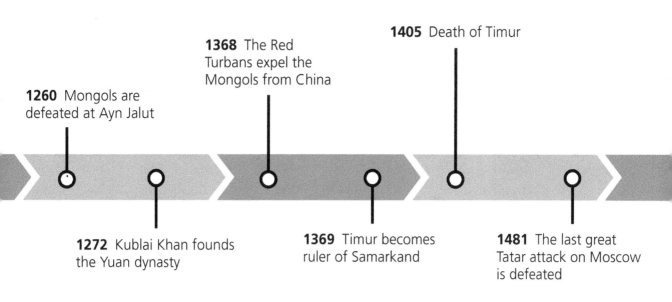

1260 Mongols are defeated at Ayn Jalut

1368 The Red Turbans expel the Mongols from China

1405 Death of Timur

1272 Kublai Khan founds the Yuan dynasty

1369 Timur becomes ruler of Samarkand

1481 The last great Tatar attack on Moscow is defeated

Key vocabulary

Tatars Name originally given to the first Mongol invaders of Europe, later applied to Mongols in Russia

Teutonic Knights German order of medieval knights who were powerful in eastern Europe

Trebuchet Very large type of catapult that uses a long arm and a counterweight to throw a projectile

Turks Ethnic group originally from central Asia, who inhabited many of the lands along the Silk Road

Yam Mongol system of postal stations that allowed messages to be relayed very quickly

Yasa Mongol law code that applied to steppe peoples throughout the Mongol domains

Yuan dynasty Mongol dynasty of Chinese emperors founded by Kublai Khan

Key people

Chinggis Khan The first Mongol conqueror, arguably the greatest warlord in the history of the world

Ivan the Great Russian emperor who united the country and defeated the Tatars

Kublai Khan Mongol khagan and Emperor of China

Möngke Khan Mongol khagan who sent a horde to conquer the Arab world

Ögedei Khan Chinggis' successor, who sent hordes to conquer Persia and Russia

Marco Polo Italian explorer who wrote a bestselling medieval book about his journey to China

Timur Lenk Ruler of Samarkand who built a great empire, remembered as the last of the Mongol conquerors

TIMELINE

400–600 The Angles and Saxons arrive in England from Germany

410 The Roman army leaves Britain

597 Augustine arrives in England to convert the Anglo-Saxons to Christianity

610 The Prophet Muhammad receives revelations from Allah

611 Completion of the Grand Canal

618 Tang dynasty established in China

632 Death of Muhammad

661 Muawiya founds the Umayyad caliphate

690 Empress Wu officially takes the throne

711 Umayyad and Berber armies invade and conquer Iberia

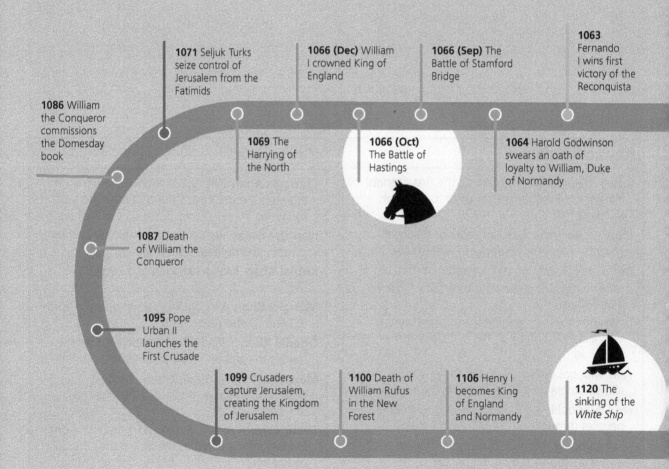

1086 William the Conqueror commissions the Domesday book

1071 Seljuk Turks seize control of Jerusalem from the Fatimids

1069 The Harrying of the North

1066 (Dec) William I crowned King of England

1066 (Oct) The Battle of Hastings

1066 (Sep) The Battle of Stamford Bridge

1064 Harold Godwinson swears an oath of loyalty to William, Duke of Normandy

1063 Fernando I wins first victory of the Reconquista

1087 Death of William the Conqueror

1095 Pope Urban II launches the First Crusade

1099 Crusaders capture Jerusalem, creating the Kingdom of Jerusalem

1100 Death of William Rufus in the New Forest

1106 Henry I becomes King of England and Normandy

1120 The sinking of the *White Ship*

731 The Venerable Bede completes *The Ecclesiastical History of the English People*

750 Abbasid caliphate established

793 The Vikings attack the monastery on Lindisfarne

865 The invasion of the 'Great Heathen Army'

732 Umayyad advance into France stopped at the Battle of Tours

762 Baghdad founded

868 The first printed book is made in China

871 Alfred the Great is crowned King of Wessex

878 Alfred the Great defeats the 'Great Heathen Army' at the Battle of Edington

1051 Edward the Confessor promises the English throne to William, Duke of Normandy

969 Fatimids take Egypt from the Abbasids

937 Æthelstan's victory at the Battle of Brunanburh confirms Anglo-Saxon rule of all England

899 Alfred the Great dies

1016 The Viking ruler Canute becomes King of England

960 Song dynasty established in China

907 Fall of the Tang dynasty

1148 The Second Crusade ends in defeat after a failed attack on the city of Damascus

1154 Henry II is crowned King of England

1170 Henry II accidently orders the murder of Thomas Becket

1187 Salah al-Din captures Jerusalem, having defeated the crusader force at the Battle of Hattin

1192 The Third Crusade ends with peace between Richard I and Salah al-Din

1135 The start of 'the Anarchy'

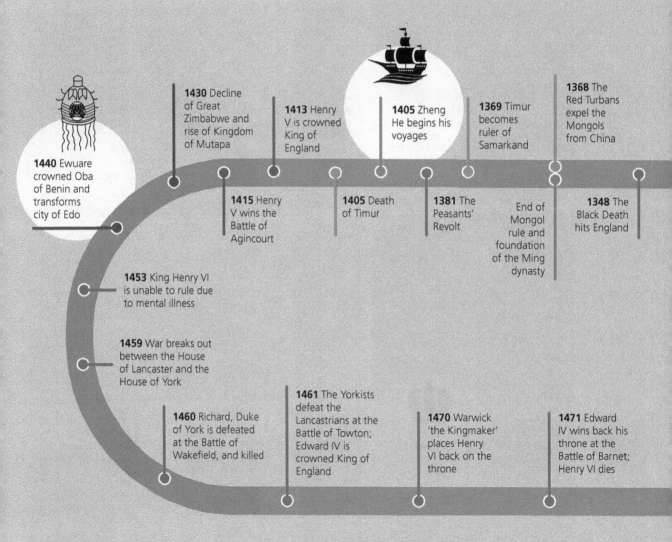

1199 King John is crowned King of England after the death of his brother Richard

1204 Eleanor of Aquitaine dies

1212 The so-called 'Children's Crusade' is thought to have left Europe for the Holy Land

1219 Chinggis invades the Khwarazmian Empire

1227 Death of Chinggis Khan

1204 The Fourth Crusade ends with the sack of Constantinople

1206 Chinggis becomes khagan of all Mongols

1215 The barons force King John to sign Magna Carta

1220 First stone structures are built at Great Zimbabwe

1440 Ewuare crowned Oba of Benin and transforms city of Edo

1430 Decline of Great Zimbabwe and rise of Kingdom of Mutapa

1413 Henry V is crowned King of England

1405 Zheng He begins his voyages

1369 Timur becomes ruler of Samarkand

1368 The Red Turbans expel the Mongols from China

1415 Henry V wins the Battle of Agincourt

1405 Death of Timur

1381 The Peasants' Revolt

End of Mongol rule and foundation of the Ming dynasty

1348 The Black Death hits England

1453 King Henry VI is unable to rule due to mental illness

1459 War breaks out between the House of Lancaster and the House of York

1461 The Yorkists defeat the Lancastrians at the Battle of Towton; Edward IV is crowned King of England

1460 Richard, Duke of York is defeated at the Battle of Wakefield, and killed

1470 Warwick 'the Kingmaker' places Henry VI back on the throne

1471 Edward IV wins back his throne at the Battle of Barnet; Henry VI dies

1235 Sundiata crowned Mansa of Mali

1236 Ögedei sends hordes to conquer Persia and Russia

1260 Mongols are defeated at Ayn Jalut

1270 House of Solomon gains the Kingdom of Aksum and establishes a new Abyssinian empire

1236 Cordoba falls to the Christian armies

1258 Hülegü begins the conquest of the Middle East

Kublai Khan founds the Yuan dynasty

1272 Edward I returns from his crusade to be crowned King of England

1277 Abu Moaheb overthrows Shirazi dynasty of the Kilwa sultanate

1279 Death of the last Song emperor after losing China to the Mongols

1326 Isabella of France deposes Edward II

1314 Amda Seyon I of Abyssina begins to double empire's territory

1305 Edward I executes the rebel Scottish leader William Wallace

1283 Edward I conquers Wales and executes Daffyd ap Gruffyd

1324 Mansa Musa's pilgrimage to Mecca

1308 Isabella of France marries Edward II

1291 The last crusader stronghold of Acre falls to Mamluk invaders, ending the Crusades

1481 The last great Tatar attack on Moscow is defeated

1483 King Richard III seizes the English throne following the death of his brother

1485 Henry Tudor wins the Battle of Bosworth and is crowned King Henry VII

1492 Fall of Granada – Reconquista of Moorish Spain complete

1502 Kingdom of Mali conquered by Kingdom of Songhai

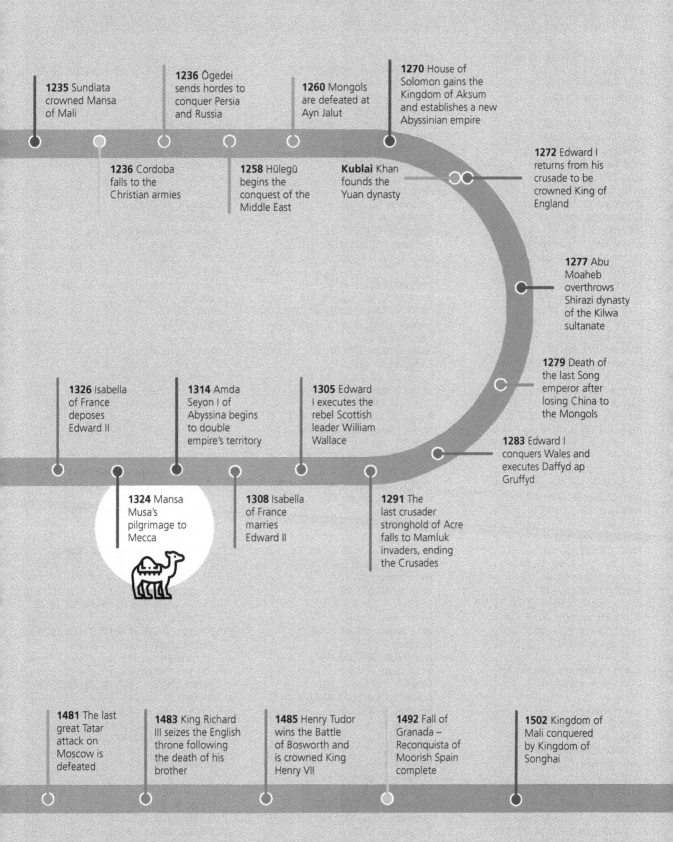

Index

Acknowledgements

Every effort has been made to trace copyright holders and to obtain their permission for the use of copyright material. The publishers will gladly receive any information enabling them to rectify any error or omission at the first opportunity. The publishers would like to thank the following for permission to reproduce copyright material:

(t = top, b = bottom, c = centre, l = left, r = right)

cover Heritage Image Partnership Ltd/Alamy, p8 Joana Kruse/Alamy, p9c World History Archive/Alamy, p9b Flik47/Shutterstock, p10 World History Archive/Alamy, p11 Heritage Image Partnership Ltd/Alamy, p12t Anna Krivitskaya/Shutterstock, p12b INTERFOTO/Alamy, p13 North Wind Pictures Archives/Alamy, p14t & 19 Awe Inspiring Images/Shutterstock, p14b Universal History Archive/UIG/Shutterstock, p15 Lebrecht Music and Arts Photo Library/Alamy, p16 Heritage Image Partnership Ltd/Alamy, p17 The Print Collector/Alamy, p20c World History Archive/Alamy, p20b Hemis/Alamy, p21 Paul Hawkett/Alamy, p22t Ian Dagnall Commercial Collection/Alamy, p22b Musée de la Tapisserie, Bayeux, France/Bridgeman Images, p23 Heritage Image Partnership Ltd/Alamy, p24 Heritage Image Partnership Ltd/Alamy, p25 Private Collection/© Look and Learn/Bridgeman Images, p26t FALKENSTEINFOTO/Alamy, p26b f8 archive/Alamy, p27 The Print Collector/Alamy, p28 Private Collection/© Look and Learn/Bridgeman Images, p29 Cotton Nero D VIII fol.7 Queen Matilda holding a charter, from the St. Alban's Chronicle (vellum), English School, (14th century) British Library, London, UK/Bridgeman Images, p30 A.C.Jones/Shutterstock, p31 Colin Underhill/Alamy, p32 North Wind Picture Archives/Alamy, p33 © British Library Board. All Rights Reserved / Bridgeman Images, p34t Daniel Dent/Shutterstock, p34b Steve Heap/Shutterstock, p35t Private Collection/© Look and Learn/Bridgeman Images, p35b robertharding/Alamy, p36 Andrew Fox/Alamy, p37t Classic Image/Alamy, p37b Sir Thomas Wriothesley, The Oxford Guide to Heraldry/Public domain/Wikimedia Commons, p38 Private Collection/© Look and Learn/Bridgeman Images, p39l Mary Evans Picture Library/Alamy, p39r Neil Mitchell/Shutterstock, p40 Private Collection/Bridgeman Images/Bridgeman Images, p41t BobJackson/Alamy, p41b Private Collection/© Look and Learn/Bridgeman Images, p43 The Protected Art Archive/Alamy Stock Photo, p44 World History Archive/Alamy, p45t Everett - Art/Shutterstock, p45b Pawel Kowalczyk/Shutterstock, p46t GL Archive/Alamy, p46b David Evison/Shutterstock, p47 GL Archive/Alamy, p48t & 54 Art Directors & TRIP/Alamy, p48b Gail Johnson/Shutterstock, p49tr douglasmack/Shutterstock, p49bl skyearth/Shutterstock, p50 & 55 World History Archive/Alamy, p51t Private Collection/© Look and Learn/Bridgeman Images, p51b Holmes Garden Photos/Alamy, p52 BRIAN HARRIS /Alamy, p53 Everett Collection Historica/Alamy, p56t Private Collection/© Look and Learn/Bridgeman Images, p56b David Kilpatrick / Alamy Stock Photo, p57 Mary Evans Picture Library/Alamy, p58 Florilegius/Alamy, p59 Derek Croucher/Alamy, p60t & 67 Private Collection/Bridgeman Images, p60c Jane Rix/Shutterstock, p60b Jane Rix/Shutterstock, p61 © Look and Learn/Bridgeman Images, p62 Everett - Art/Shutterstock, p63t Salparadis/Shutterstock, p63b Pictorial Press Ltd/Alamy, p64t Georgios Kollidas/Alamy, p64b Lanmas/Alamy, p65c © Walker Art Gallery, National Museums Liverpool/Bridgeman Images, p65b David Warren/Alamy, p68t Mikhail Priakhin/Shutterstock, p68b KiyechkaSo/Shutterstock, p69 TEA OOR/Shutterstock, p70t North Wind Picture Archives/Alamy Stock Photo, p70b mohammad alzain/Shutterstock, p71 The Print Collector / Alamy Stock Photo, p72 Aleksander Todorovic/Shutterstock, p73c Sergey Melnikov/Shutterstock, p73b Science History Images/Alamy, p74 Abd Al Kader Azar/Shutterstock, p75t abdelfatah/Shutterstock, p75b NickolayV/Shutterstock, p76 Sean Pavone/Shutterstock, p77 Heritage Image Partnership Ltd/Alamy Stock Photo, p80t Mikhail Markovskiy/Shutterstock, p80c Victor Lauer/Shutterstock, p80b Aleksander Todorovic/Shutterstock, p81 Private Collection/© Look and Learn/Bridgeman Images, p82t Anton_Ivanov/Shutterstock, p82b Mikhail Markovskiy/Shutterstock, p83 Vintage Library / Alamy, p84 Tony Baggett/Shutterstock, p85t Ilia Torlin/Shutterstock, p85b Boda Art Works/Shutterstock, p86 ASP Religion/Alamy, p87 ASP Religion/Alamy, p88 dinomischail/Shutterstock, p89 Robert Hoetink/Shutterstock, p91 Greg Balfour Evans/Alamy, p92 Matej Hudovernik/Shutterstock, p93t Artush/Shutterstock, p93c Matyas Rehak/Shutterstock, p95t incamerastock/Alamy, p95b Marianoblanco/Shutterstock, p96 CPA Media Pte Ltd / Alamy Stock Photo, p97c Everett Collection/Shutterstock, p97b Heritage Image Partnership Ltd/Alamy, p98t Album / Alamy Stock Photo, p98b evenfh/Shutterstock, p99 Jo Reason/Shutterstock , p100t Robin Batista/Shutterstock , p100b Pictures From History / Alamy Stock Photo, p101t travelview/Shutterstock , p101b Seashell world/Shutterstock, p104 incamerastock/Alamy, p105 dajingjing/Shutterstock, p106b Alina Martina Madarasz/Shutterstock, p107t Everett Collection/Shutterstock, p107b Yingna Cai/Shutterstock, p108t JIANG TIANMU/Shutterstock, p108b The Print Collector/Alamy, p109t cl2004lhy/Shutterstock, p109b Shan_shan/Shutterstock, p110 Charlesimage/Shutterstock, p111t CPA Media Pte Ltd/Alamy, p111b & 114 The Art Archive/Shutterstock, p112 Dr. Victor Wong/Shutterstock, p113c Sobeautiful/Shutterstock, p113b aphotostory/Shutterstock, p116 IanDagnall Computing/Alamy, p117 Dmitry Chulov/Shutterstock, p118 INTERFOTO / History / Alamy Stock Photo, p119t worldroadtrip/Shutterstock, p119b Arctic Phoenix/Shutterstock, p120 beibaoke/Shutterstock, p121 Chronicle of World History/Alamy, p122 Dudarev Mikhail/Shutterstock, p123t Katiekk/Shutterstock, p123b beibaoke/Shutterstock, p124 Tim Graham/Alamy, p125t monticello/Shutterstock, p125b Elena Koromyslova/Shutterstock.